ANNE OF THE THOUSAND DAYS

BY MAXWELL ANDERSON

★

★

DRAMATISTS
PLAY SERVICE
INC.

ANNE OF THE THOUSAND DAYS was first presented by The Playwrights' Company and Leland Hayward at the Shubert Theatre, New York City, on December 8, 1948, with a cast featuring Joyce Redman as Anne Boleyn and Rex Harrison as Henry the Eighth. Settings were by Jo Mielziner, Costumes by Motley, Incidental Music by Lehman Engel, Staged by H. C. Potter.

ANNE BOLEYN
HENRY THE EIGHTH
CARDINAL WOLSEY
THOMAS BOLEYN
HENRY NORRIS
MARK SMEATON
DUKE OF NORFOLK
LORD PERCY, *Earl of Northumberland*
ELIZABETH BOLEYN
MARY BOLEYN
SIR THOMAS MORE
MADGE SHELTON
JANE SEYMOUR
BISHOP FISHER
JOHN HOUGHTON
THOMAS CROMWELL

There are several servants, most of whom can be doubled in several scenes; 3 musicians, 3 choir boys, 2 bailiffs, Clerk of the Court and a few extra courtiers.

The scenes are in and just outside of various palaces in London, also Windsor Palace and the Tower of London. (For explanation of the settings, see Production Note.)

PRODUCTION NOTE

The present acting edition of ANNE OF THE THOUSAND DAYS is that used in the original New York production. The nonprofessional director will soon realize in reading the present text that he is allowed very considerable liberty in setting and background.

The play is definitely a play of memory. As originally conceived by the author, it consisted of brief scenes, moments remembered by Anne and Henry of their short-lived courtship and marriage. Memories that concern intimate relationships usually picture the individuals quite clearly, but often leave the background a blur. That is the impression Mr. Anderson wished to create in this play. He wanted his characters to be real people such as one would meet anywhere today, using the same language and speaking naturally as we do. But the background, other than being vaguely Tudor, should be almost undefinable. The actors should be figures moving in and out of light. As produced by The Playwrights' in New York, a single setting sufficed. It suggested a castle, either interior or exterior, with an arch center, an arch R. C., and a circular stairway L. C., disappearing behind the set. The whole enclosed in a huge cyclorama. Henry delivered his soliloquies from L. 1, sitting at a small desk or table. The only light a single spot. Anne spoke from R. 1, sitting on a pedestal at the base of a flat that was swung out in the darkness. She, too, had a single spot, but on the flat above her a projection of prison bars suggested "The Tower." Projections were played on the central set to indicate the Chapel, windows for interior scenes, leaves for outdoor scenes and prison bars for the trial scene. The many scenes were tied together with interludes of music, just a few bars to change the mood from one scene to the next, and allow time for the stage-hands to change the few necessary properties in the darkness. The musical instruments used were harp, cello, two violins and horn.

While the musical instruments just mentioned were actually used onstage, it is, of course, not necessary that musicians be actually employed for nonprofessional productions. The same effect can be secured by the use of phonograph records. While the music played should, of course, not be modern in mood or spirit, there is no necessity that it should actually be English music dating from Tudor days. The point to be emphasized is that this music should be simple, and should have no hint in it of modern orchestration or harmony. Doubt-

4

less, any classic music from the period of Bach or earlier would be appropriate.

Throughout the text of this edition, entrances and exits are indicated as " R. 1," " R. 2," and " U. R."; " L. 1," " L. 2," and " U. L." The numerals 1 and 2 indicate respectively down-stage and about half-way between down and upstage, either L. or R. The letter " U." indicates upstage. For several of the scenes, there are two very simple arches (actually intended to suggest doorways or entrances) about center-stage, and the suggestion of a simple stairway from L. of the center arch, going up a few steps. All changes of furniture are made during the blackout between the scenes.

Thanks are hereby tendered to Mr. Maury Tuckerman, Assistant Stage Manager of the New York production of ANNE OF THE THOUSAND DAYS, for considerable help and advice in connection with the preparation of the present acting script.

ANNE OF THE THOUSAND DAYS

ACT I

PROLOGUE

Curtain rises on darkness. A single spot comes up disclosing ANNE *seated* R. 1. *Bars of " The Tower " indicated above her.* HENRY *sits in darkness at his desk* L. 1. *Preset for* SCENE 1, *a chair and small table* L. C.

ANNE.

If I were to die now—
but I must not die yet,
not yet.
It's been too brief. A few weeks and days.
How many days, I wonder, since the first time
I gave myself, to that last day when he—
when he left me at the lists and I saw him no more?
Well, I can reckon it.
I have time enough. Those who sit in the Tower
don't lack for time.

He could never cipher.
He was shrewd and heavy—
and cunning with his tongue, and wary in intrigue,
but when it came to adding up an account
he filled it with errors and bit his tongue—
and swore—
till I slapped his hands like a child and took the pen
and made it straight.
" A king," I said, " a king, and cannot reckon."
I was his clever girl then, his Nan;
he'd kiss me then, and maul me, and take me down.

7

On the rushes. Anywhere.
Why do I think of it now? Would he kill me? Kill me?
Henry? The fool? That great fool kill me?

Could I kill him, I wonder?
I feel it in my hands perhaps I could.
So—perhaps he could kill me.—
Perhaps he could kill me.

If I die now, I go out into night,
and Elizabeth, my firstling, all I have,
must face the new world in the morning.
To those who die we seem to go forward into darkness.
To those who are new-born we seem to go forward into
dawn.
As I bore Elizabeth, midnight will bear morning.
(*A single spot comes up showing* HENRY *at his desk* L. 1.)
HENRY.

This is hard to do
when you come to put pen to paper.
You say to yourself:
She must die. And she must—
if things are to go as planned.
Yes, if they are to go at all.
If I am to rule
and keep my sanity and hold my England off the rocks.
It's a lee shore—and a low tide—and the wind's a gale—
and the Spanish rocks are bare and sharp.
(ANNE'S *spot fades slowly out.*)
Go back to it, Henry, go back to it.
Keep your mind
on this parchment you must sign.
Dip the pen in the ink; write your name.

You've condemned men, nobles and peasants.
She's struck down a few herself—
or driven you to it.
It's only that a woman you've held in your arms
and longed for when she was away,

8

and suffered with her—no, but she promised you an heir.
Write it down—
Write Henry Rex, and it's done.
And then the headsman
will cry out suddenly, " Look, look there! "
(He points suddenly offstage.)
and point to the first flash of sunrise,
and she'll look,
not knowing what he means, and his sword will flash
in the flick of sun, through the little bones of her neck
as she looks away,
and it will be done.
It will be done.
How did I come to this?
What were you like, Henry,
when she flashed her first anger at you
ten years ago in Spring?
How hopeful were you,
how mistaken, then,
how ridiculous,
how much in love?

SLOW BLACKOUT

(ANNE'S *seat and* HENRY'S *desk removed during blackout.*)

SCENE 2

Hever Castle. A room. Enter WOLSEY *and* BOLEYN. *Lights come up as scene begins.*

BOLEYN. This way, my lord, Cardinal.
WOLSEY. The King rode close behind me, Thomas.
BOLEYN. And he comes to see Anne, not Mary?
WOLSEY. He comes to see Anne, not Mary.
BOLEYN. My lord, I'm in a most peculiar position here. My daughter Mary has been the King's mistress for four years. The whole world knows it. Now the king comes asking for my daugh-

ter Anne. What am I to say to Mary? And what am I to say to Anne?

WOLSEY. Tell her, in plain words, that the King wants her.

BOLEYN. My dear Cardinal, I have encouraged Anne with the Earl of Northumberland. He'll have the greatest estates in the North of England. It never entered my head that the King had noticed her. What can I say to her now?

WOLSEY. To send the Earl away.

BOLEYN. I think they have a sort of engagement between them. (*Trumpet call.*)

WOLSEY. Well, the King's here.

BOLEYN. I think it will need more time.

WOLSEY. Suppose you take the King to look at your hounds. Tell him that Anne had ordered a new dress and there's some trouble with it—her hands tremble over the fastenings, and other rubbish of that sort ——

BOLEYN. The King knows when you're talking to fill time, and he cuts through it.

WOLSEY. Nonsense, there's a whole list of baits he'll snap at. Speak of poetry and he'll recite his latest poem to you. Speak of music and he'll sing you a song of his own composing, speak of hunting and he'll tell you how to kill a deer and cook it, speak of women ——

BOLEYN Yes?

WOLSEY. No, don't mention women. We must leave here before noon tomorrow.—I'll speak to Anne and to the Earl.

BOLEYN. Well, if you can manage it. I'm her father and I don't know how to go about it.

SERVANT. (*Entering* C. *arch.*) My lord! My lord! (NORRIS *and* SMEATON *enter, followed by* HENRY, C. *arch.*)

HENRY. (*To* NORRIS *and* SMEATON.) Wait for me, gentlemen. Only your king, Thomas. No ceremony. Only your Henry. (NORRIS *goes out* U. R., SMEATON U. L., SERVANT L. 1. HENRY *extends hand to* THOMAS, *anyway. To* WOLSEY.) And how's the vicar of hell this chilly Spring morning?

WOLSEY. I keep warm, Majesty.

HENRY. I'm sure you do. With your feet on the devil's fender. Meanwhile toasting your paddocks at God's altar.

WOLSEY. And running the King's errands. It's a busy life.

HENRY. Has he done my errand?

BOLEYN. Yes, he has.

HENRY. May I smell this pretty posy of yours?

BOLEYN. My lord, if you mean Anne, could you give her a half hour? She's still at her mirror.

HENRY. We've this whole day ——

BOLEYN. There was a clump of red deer grazing within view when I last looked out. In velvet, but they give promise of sport later.

HENRY. We'll see them. We'll see your red deer, and afterward we'll appraise what was seen in that same looking-glass.

WOLSEY. Good hunting, Majesty.

HENRY. You won't be with us?

WOLSEY. It happens there is a poor soul in the house who seeks the ministrations of a religious. I must go where I am called.

HENRY. You will go wherever it's most profitable for the Cardinal of York to be at any given time. So go there, and no more of these holy thin excuses.

WOLSEY. Yes, Majesty. (*Exit* WOLSEY R. 1.)

HENRY. There's no hurry about the deer. I want three words with you.

BOLEYN. Yes? My lord!

HENRY. There's always a temptation when a man's in my position that he'll think of the nation as his own trough, and get all four feet in it and eat from one end to the other. I don't want to look like that to anybody.

BOLEYN. You don't, my sovereign.

HENRY. I'm a religious man, Boleyn. I want to do what's right in the eyes of God and the church. And myself—and my people—and you.

BOLEYN. That's a swath of folk to satisfy—if you include God.

HENRY. I include both God and the women—among them your daughters. What will your daughters say of me—the two of them together—talking at night? Um?

BOLEYN. What two women say together—talking at night of one man who has wanted them both—and taken both—no man will ever know that.—But I think—if you don't mind ——

HENRY. I've asked you.

BOLEYN. I think you go a little rapid with Annie. You'll need to be gentle.

HENRY. But she'll have me—in the end?

BOLEYN. She's no fool, my lord.

HENRY. (*After a pause.*) What I do is God's will.

BOLEYN. Now, if a man or a monarch could be sure of that.

HENRY.

> I've worked it out, in my mind.—
> I pray to God.
> I tell you this first, Boleyn.
> God answers prayer. That's known. Every morning I go on
>   my knees
> and pray that what I do may be God's will.
> I pray him to direct me—that whatever thought
> comes to my mind—whatever motion
> floods in my heart—shall be God's will—and I
> only his instrument. Wherever I turn,
> whatever I do—whether to reach for food,
> or thread my way among the crossed paths of the law,
> or interpret the holy word,
> or judge men innocent—or guilty—
> every morning I pray Him on my knees
> nothing shall rise in my brain or heart but He
> has wished it first.
> And since He answers prayer,
> and since He's given me such heavy power to act,
> power for good and evil,
> He must answer this. He does answer.
> I find such peace in this,
> that not one morning my whole life long
> shall I fail these devotions.

BOLEYN. This is a noble thought, of course, but Your Majesty realizes that it might be used as an excuse for ——

HENRY. For what?

BOLEYN. For doing as you please.

HENRY. I'm quite serious, Boleyn. I want no trifling . . .

BOLEYN. It was not my intention to trifle.

HENRY. But you do. I tell you I pray and God answers.

BOLEYN. Yes, my lord.

HENRY.

> I am younger than you. I am younger than Wolsey.
> I am younger than many dukes and earls and peers.
> But I am the King of England. When I pray God answers.
> I will not have this questioned.

12

BOLEYN. Yes, my lord. (NORRIS *and* SMEATON *enter* C. *arch.*)

NORRIS. We're sent as a delegation, my lord.

HENRY. Come in, come in. Pour it on, whatever it is. Your King is your natural receptacle for whatever you can't hold any longer.

NORRIS. The fact is we are sent to keep you amused while Sir Thomas Boleyn confers with his lady wife.

SMEATON. There is a sort of kitchen rebellion afoot and his voice is needed.

HENRY. Go, Boleyn, mollify your women.

BOLEYN. If you'll excuse me. (*Exit* BOLEYN C. *arch.*)

HENRY. I want a word with you, anyway—man to man, kingship aside. You buzz the girls, you two—you've thrust your hands in amongst a flutter of larks often enough and pulled out the one you wanted. Tell me, what's the best cast of all for a maiden?

SMEATON. A maid, Your Majesty?

HENRY. I wouldn't swear to that. Not medically. But a young one—a bit wild—uncaught.

NORRIS. I couldn't say of my own knowledge, sir, but Tom Wyatt has an unfailing way. He writes them poems.

SMEATON. But you can't catch a ticklish hoyden with madrigals. That's for matrons.

HENRY. Then your lure, Smeaton? Your favorite?

SMEATON. My King, my acquaintance doesn't run among the grade of females you seek. I'm more successful with waiting women and ladies' maids.

HENRY. Don't be modest, lad. I've followed your spoor so close there was scarce time to close the window you left by—or change perfumes to put me off the scent ——

SMEATON. Truly, truly ——

HENRY. I've breathed your same air in some close quarters, singer. So speak on. Your lure? Your most seductive.

SMEATON. Why, being a singer, I sing to them a good deal—but, in addition to that—you will not be offended?

HENRY. I'll be offended if you keep back, musician.

SMEATON. Why, then, if you truly want her, make her believe you're potent only with her, Majesty, and that will do the business. Make out that you've tried with numbers of others, gone to bed and kissed hotly, and hung embarrassed and unable. But with her you rouse up. You're a man again. They can't resist that. They open like ——

13

HENRY. Never mind the simile. There's nothing like it. But, lad, this is new, this device.

SMEATON. I think it's my own.

HENRY. And ingenious. (NORFOLK *enters* C. *arch.*)

NORFOLK. May an old man intrude among the lads?

HENRY. Norfolk! We're speaking of the best way to woo a green maid. You're a man of expedients. You know these things—if you haven't forgotten them.

NORFOLK. Why, my advice is, if you want a woman, take her.

HENRY. There are certain preliminaries. There's consent, anyway. You must have consent.

NORFOLK. Nonsense. Take her and make her like it. Why should a woman have anything to say about it?

HENRY. It may have been so in the good old days. Today we woo —and wait.

NORRIS. Do you wish her to be in love with you, my lord?

HENRY. That I do.

NORRIS. Do you wish to be in love with her?

HENRY. In love with her? I? Personally? Now, I'll tell you the truth, so far my experience of being in love is like this: love is a kind of wanting, a panting and sighing and longing. What does a man desire of a lass, anyway? To be assuaged. He wants his pain assuaged. Well, that done, what more's to be done?

SMEATON. Is it lèse majesté, or may I ask ——?

HENRY. Nothing is lèse majesté in this conversation ——

SMEATON. Have you ever been refused by a maid?

HENRY. Refused? I? No, I think not. When I've wanted them I've had them. And once I've had a wench, I'm cured. That's general, isn't it? Broad and narrow?

NORRIS. My King, with me it's the opposite. Once I've mixed flesh and lips with her I'm in danger of a golden wedding—should we both live.

HENRY. It can happen so?

SMEATON. The poor gudgeon's hooked now. He'll never swim free again.

NORRIS. And she won't look at me.

HENRY. Keep me from that, good God!

NORFOLK. Can Your Majesty leave talking of virgins long enough to look at the venison?

14

HENRY. Yes—come. Next to the haunch of a virgin there's nothing like a haunch of venison. (*All start to exit* C. *arch.*)

BLACKOUT

(*Chair and table removed, replaced by a bench* L. C.)

SCENE 3

Exterior of Hever Castle. Lights come up as scene starts. Projection of moonlight through leaves all over set.

PERCY. (*Calling as he enters* U. L.) Anne! Anne! Annie!

ANNE. (*Offstage* R. 2.) I'm coming!

PERCY. You said you'd be here when the moonlight touched the West chimney. And you're not here. Are you angry with me?

ANNE. (*Running on stage* R. 2 *and into his arms.*) Yes, I'm terribly angry.

PERCY. You are so?

ANNE. No, of course not. I'm angry with myself.

PERCY. Yes, dear.

ANNE. I'm angry with myself about one thing. I spent two years at the court of Queen Claude. I met there the silkened flower of the aristocracy. Such manners, such grace, such horsemanship and dancing! They spoke Greek, they spoke Latin, they spoke Italian —and they spoke their own French with a wit and a fencer's point that gave me a glimpse of what a language could be!

PERCY. But what disappointed you?

ANNE. Among them there were—well, truly gallant men. Captivating men. Charmers. With an ease of carriage—and a way with women that —— And I fell in love with none of them. I came home and promptly fell in love with a—a thistle. A countryman from the North. With no graces at all. Can't dance. Can't sing. Can hardly speak English.

PERCY. Can put his arm around you.

ANNE. Doesn't do that well. Not as well as I've known it done. But it's the one arm I want—for some God-knows-what reason.

15

You do everything badly—everything awkwardly—and I love it the way you do it.

PERCY. I'm glad I wasn't educated in France.

ANNE. Why?

PERCY. You wouldn't have loved me.

ANNE. I wonder. It may be true.

PERCY. Silks are for holiday. Honest homespun wears through the years.

ANNE. One thing, though. If we love enough to marry we must love enough to keep nothing back. I shall keep nothing from you.

PERCY. Nor I from you, sweet.

ANNE. But you have. You don't know what I mean.

PERCY. Are we to lie together? Before?

ANNE. If you like. But that's not it.

PERCY. My bonny, what more can there be than that?

ANNE. Kiss me hard. (*He kisses her.*)

PERCY. I wish I had you in my house.

ANNE. (*Musing.*) That's part of it, too, and to be Lady Anne, and live with you in your house, and sleep with you at night. Tell me, are you a virgin?

PERCY. I?

ANNE. Yes, Earl of Northumberland—you.

PERCY. I'm a man.

ANNE. I know. But are you a virgin? When we bed together shall I be your first?

PERCY. I ——

ANNE. Don't be confused, dear. We don't come out of a rainbow at seventeen and there's no use pretending we did. You may ask me whatever you like. (*A pause.*)

PERCY. Are you a virgin?

ANNE. No.

PERCY. Was this something that happened in France?

ANNE. Yes. But long before France, too. (*She rises.*) God help me, I'm blushing. I thought I'd finished with that. But no—it began at my heels—I could feel it—and rushed up in a wave till now it burns at the roots of my hair. And I've told this before ——

PERCY. Without blushing?

ANNE. (*Defiantly.*) Yes! But there's something in the foggy, torpid air of this island that makes people want to hide things. Like savages.

PERCY. There might be another reason.

ANNE. What?

PERCY. Look at me. (*She does so.*) Were you ever in love before?

ANNE. No!

PERCY. Now I'm no spring of wisdom in these matters, Anne, but it may be you're not a woman till you're in love. It may be you've nothing to hide till then.

ANNE. (*Slowly.*) Yes. It may be. It may be that you're wiser than you think.

PERCY. I hope so. A man has to be wiser than he thinks or he won't go far. I'm afraid I don't like this game you learned in Paris.

ANNE. Were you an angel, darling?

PERCY. No. I was not.

ANNE. Tell me about the girls. How many, and when!

PERCY. One thing you'd best learn now, my sweet. I'll be the man of the house when we have a house, and if any game's to be played I'll lead in that game and not follow. The game I like now is to put my arms about you and say nothing.

ANNE. You know, I think I like that better, too.

PERCY. Come, then. (PERCY *takes* ANNE *in his arms again. At the same moment* WOLSEY *enters* R. *arch, and* ANNE *puts up a hand to hold* PERCY'S *lips from hers.*)

ANNE. The Cardinal is here. (WOLSEY *steps toward them into the light.*)

PERCY. Cardinal Wolsey!

WOLSEY. I'm glad I find you together, for I have to speak to you both. I'm sorry to find you so intimate, for it's about that I have to speak to you. My lord, your father and the King have given some thought to where you shall marry, and an alliance with the Talbots, through one of the daughters of the Earl of Shrewsbury, is thought best.

PERCY. An—alliance with ——! Not by me, my lord Cardinal.

WOLSEY. Anne, my dear, your father has a claim on the Ormond estates in Ireland. He and the King have agreed that you will marry the Earl of Ormond to re-enforce that claim.

ANNE. I—marry into Ireland?

WOLSEY. It's so decided.

ANNE. But how can you ——? It's not so decided! Not one word of this has been said to me! Of Ormond or Ireland ——!

WOLSEY. Your father will deal with you. As for Lord Percy, remember, if you will, that I brought you to court, and that you are still a member of my household. A half-grown steer and a leggy girl will not be allowed to overturn the policies of England, fixed in council.

PERCY. But, my lord, I am of full age, and I have pledged myself to this girl before many witnesses—among them her own father! It's a good match for both of us, and nothing's been said against it till this moment! More than that, we've pledged ourselves to each other, and our hearts go with that pledge!

WOLSEY. No doubt. And this is the reward I get for my kindness to you. (*He turns away.*)

ANNE. (*Softly.*) My lord Cardinal, that we two are in love, and have been these two months, every servant in the house knows, for we've made no secret of it before them or anyone. Why you've come here now to tell us suddenly that we're to match elsewhere, we don't know. There must be some reason behind it. Tell us what it is.

WOLSEY. I have told you.

ANNE. Then you talk nonsense, and I won't listen!

PERCY. Nor I!

WOLSEY. I stand here as the King's minister, and you're aware of that. I knew a great lord to die for less than you have just said. His name was Buckingham.

PERCY. (*More humbly.*) You know I have no wish to anger the King. But tell us what this means and why you say it to us.

WOLSEY. (*Thundering.*) Do you think the King and I come lightly to such decisions as this? Do you think we have not weighed every reason for and against before we issue a command? One thing I can tell you, you will obey or your estates are forfeit! If you continue disloyal it's doubtful how long you will live! Go now, for I wish to speak to Anne alone.

PERCY. Anne ——

ANNE. Yes, you must go.

PERCY. Kiss me, then.

WOLSEY. Do not touch her.

PERCY. All this talk of sudden death makes it very easy for you, my lord. But I shall kiss her if I like. (*And he does so.*)

ANNE. Only take care of yourself. I shall see you.

PERCY. Yes. (*He turns and goes L. 2. ANNE stands silent and defiant, looking at WOLSEY.*)

WOLSEY. Look your knives through and through me, mistress. At my age it will do me no hurt—and at yours, though you hurt easily, you will cure quickly. Are you serious about this thorn-apple from the North?

ANNE. My lord—he's mine—and I'm his.

WOLSEY. But if there were another and worthier, well, you could change?

ANNE. I want no other. And if you do him harm—this my chosen husband—I am only a girl, but you will know you have an enemy!

WOLSEY. Look down at your necklace, Anne. Do you see a writing on it?

ANNE. There's no writing on it.

WOLSEY. There is, though, and I can see it, though it may not be visible to you as yet. The writing is a quotation from a poem. It says:

"Noli me tangere. Cæsar's I am."

You have studied Latin?

ANNE. Yes.

WOLSEY. "Touch me not," the translation might go, "I belong to the king."

ANNE. (*After a pause.*) Forgive me if I seem slow to understand what you say. Do you mean that King Henry has looked at me?

WOLSEY. Yes.

ANNE. And sent you to me?

WOLSEY. It is sometimes my pleasure to anticiate his desires.

ANNE. Perhaps you would be wise to anticipate the answer he will receive from me if he comes. We have had him in the bosom of our family for some years. My sister Mary is probably with child by him at the moment. And of no further use to him. I shall not go the way of my sister, thank you —— (THOMAS BOLEYN *and his wife,* ELIZABETH, *enter* L. 2.)

BOLEYN. Anne!

ANNE. Do you also offer me up to this royal bull—you, my father? And you, my mother?

BOLEYN. Hush, daughter! Manage your voice. He's in the house.

ANNE. Why is he here?

BOLEYN. To see you.

ANNE. Well—you've let him come—I haven't. Find some way out of it.

BOLEYN. It's not my doing. It's his. He came quite openly demand·

ing you. And since that is what every girl in England prays for, how was I to know it would displease you?

ANNE. Do you know what it is to be in love? Either of you? Do you remember? Remember what it's like to have your whole life follow one person out at the door—and not to live again, and not want to live, till he returns?

BOLEYN. You have been in France—and at the court.

ANNE. I've been many places, and done more things than you know—yet there's only one man I want now! And I'll have no one else! No one! Mother!

ELIZABETH. Yes—I said these things once—all of them—and I would help you now if I could. But I know now that we're not free to have or take or choose. You are here—and you live—and we all of us live—because we took advantage when it came our way, because we stood at the door and waited, because we smiled where a smile would help, and kissed when a kiss would help ——

ANNE. My lord Cardinal, we are only one family among many at court—and in this family only two sisters, Mary and I. Surely one of two sisters should be enough. Surely he could look else-where now.

WOLSEY. There are only these things to blame—the King's will, and your own self, your form and face and words. The King has seen you and heard your voice and liked you. I can't change that.

HENRY. (*Heard offstage.*) You there! Kindly inquire if the King may enter!

WOLSEY. And I can't change him.

HENRY. (*Still unseen.*) Right! Right! I speak to you! A sovereign has so little privacy that he knows how to respect the privacy of others. So ask! Inquire!

SERVANT. (*Entering* R. *arch.*) May the King approach?

HENRY. (*Entering* R. *arch.*) That says it. That puts it bluntly. A good honest half-witted serving-man you have here, if ever I saw one. Aren't you, fellow?

SERVANT. If Your Majesty please, yes, Sire. (*Bows and exits* U. R.)

BOLEYN. Your Majesty knows that you are always welcome in this house.

HENRY. As you in mine, Sir Thomas. And now my manners. I have greeted all here, I think, save only the lady Anne. Sweet Nan, will you give me a kiss?

ANNE. Yes, Your Majesty. (*He comes forward with his arms*

20

jovially outstretched. ANNE *bows, then takes one of his hands, kisses it coolly.*)

HENRY. It was not such a kiss I meant, my dear.

ANNE. I have been drinking foul medicine for a cold, my lord. You would never forgive my breath.

HENRY. Have you tried hippocras, a strong glassful every hour, steaming hot?

ANNE. No, I haven't.

HENRY. You shall have some of my own brewing. I'll send it to-day. For your health is very dear to me, sweet Nan, and you must keep well. We live all too brief a time—and what little we have should not be wasted in sickness. (*He stoops suddenly and kisses her.*) There is neither fever nor medicine on your lips, sweetheart, but such a honey scent as bashful maidens breathe.—Shall I send away this chaperonage that rings us round?

ANNE. No.

HENRY. I will, though, by your leave; no, without your leave. Mothers, fathers, churchmen, all these may depart. (WOLSEY *and the* BOLEYNS, THOMAS *and* ELIZABETH, *bow out backward,* WOLSEY U. L., *the* BOLEYNS L. 2.) You would never credit how fast my heart beats, nor how hard it is to draw breath. A king is not fortunate in these matters, Nan. I come to you as frightened as a 'prentice who takes his first nosegay to a wench—but whether you like me or not—whether any woman likes me or not—I shall never know. I shall never be sure I have the truth—because I am the King, and love is paid to me like taxes.—Do me this favor, Nan. Look on me not as a monarch who commands and may demand, but as the doubting, hoping, tremulous man I am—wishing to be loved for myself.

ANNE. If you were a common man, doubtful of yourself, and tremulous, would you have sent an ambassador to warn me and make sure of me?

HENRY. Did I send an ambassador?

ANNE. Wolsey speaks for you, I believe.

HENRY. Has he spoken clumsily?

ANNE. No, very deftly. He made it plain that what the King wanted he would have.

HENRY. Then he was clumsy. I swear to you, Nan, only this very cruel thing has happened to me: I have fallen in love. I tried to argue myself out of it, but seeing you day by day here, and trying not to see you, not to think about you, I have tangled myself deeper day by day, till now I can't keep it to myself. I must tell you. And ask your pity.—The truth is I dared not speak to you first myself. I was afraid.

ANNE. You were afraid?

HENRY. Yes.

ANNE. Of what?

HENRY. That you wouldn't care for me.

ANNE. Then perhaps you will understand the very cruel thing that has happened to me: I have fallen in love.—And not with you.

HENRY. By God!

ANNE. You were complaining a moment ago that such remarks were not made to kings.

HENRY. By God, I got it full in the face that time!—Who is it? Northumberland?

ANNE. Would I be wise to tell you?

HENRY. Never mind. I know. I've been told but I didn't believe it. How far has it gone?

ANNE. We mean to be married.

HENRY. Yes?

ANNE. But not as my sister's married. He would not be a complaisant husband—and I would not be an accessible wife.

HENRY. All wives are accessible—any husband can be placated.

ANNE. Not all.

HENRY. Yes, all! But I don't want you that way! Damn my soul and yours—I've heard tales of this. I've told lies about it, but I never thought to feel the blade in my own vitals! I don't want you that way! I want you to myself!

ANNE. What can I do?

HENRY.

    Give up this young wattle-and-daub—
    give him up, I tell you,
    and this kingdom shall turn around you, bishops and
    peers—
    and whatever you've wanted, for anyone,
    a knighthood,
    an estate, a great income rolling in forever,
    titles and places, you shall dispose of them
    just as you please!

ANNE.

> And be thrown out in the end
> like a dirty rag.—I haven't seen Mary disposing
> of revenues.

HENRY.

> She asked for nothing. Look, Anne,
> I'm here desperate. I can't bargain with you.
> Ask for what you want.

ANNE.

> To be free. To be free
> to marry where I love.

(HENRY *pauses*.)

HENRY

> No.

ANNE.

> I too can say no!
> I've seen you too close
> and known you too long. I've heard what your court-
> iers say,
> and then I've seen what you are. You're spoiled and
> vengeful,
> and malicious and bloody. The poetry they praise
> so much is sour, and the music you write's worse.
> You dance like a hobbledehoy; you make love
> as you eat—with a good deal of noise and no
> subtlety.
> It was my doubtful pleasure once to sleep in Mary's
> room—
> or to lie awake when you thought me asleep, and observe
> the royal porpoise at play—

HENRY.

> This is not safe.

ANNE.

> Yes, I've been told it's not safe for any of us
> to say no to our squire Harry. This put-on, kindly
> hail-fellow-well-met of yours. My father's house
> will be pulled down—and Northumberland's, too,
> they tell me.
> Well, pull them down. You are what I said.

HENRY.

    I had no wish to come here. I came
because I must, and couldn't help myself.
Well—I'm well out of it. Let it end here tonight.
I thank you for your anger,
and for raising anger in me. There's no better way
to make an end.—Wolsey! Where's the fat saddle-bags?

ANNE.

    You will not—touch—Northumberland?

HENRY.

    I'll try not.
Vengeful as I am, I'll try not.
(He calls.)
Wolsey!
(He goes out C. *arch.)*
Where's this vicar of hell?
(ANNE *falls* C. *stage in a dead faint.)*

BLACKOUT

(Bench removed in blackout.)

SCENE 4

Interior of Hever Castle. ELIZABETH *and* NORFOLK *discovered as lights go up.* ELIZABETH *signals two servants to bring on table and two chairs from* R. 2.

ELIZABETH. We'll do what we can—but tonight ——

NORFOLK. The King wants it all set up as if for a little play.

ELIZABETH. How many are with him?

NORFOLK. His singers and musicians.—There's no arguing with him. What he wants, he wants.

ELIZABETH. And who is to be in the audience?

NORFOLK. Only the Boleyn family, I gather.

ELIZABETH. The Boleyn family . . . Nan still sits in her room, you know.

NORFOLK. But she'll appear tonight.

24

ELIZABETH. I don't know, brother. It's been two years since she quarrelled with the King, and much has happened. She's not the same girl. I have no influence over her, nor has her father.

NORFOLK. But since Northumberland's dead—what does she wait for?

ELIZABETH. I don't know. (*A* SERVANT *enters* L. *with music stand —and one from* R. *with two stools.*) We'll place the musicians here, I think, and the singers can stand on the steps. Those who listen can sit on this side.—Must it be this evening . . . instantly?

NORFOLK. Without delay! (*Exit* SERVANTS.)

ELIZABETH. When that letter came—and Northumberland had been married off to the Shrewsbury horror, Anne spoke to no one, you know. Not even to me. She stayed in her room. I think that marriage killed Northumberland. And it came near to killing Anne. She takes no interest in us.—She takes no part in what goes on in the house. (MARY BOLEYN *enters* C. *arch.*) She reads, and stares at the wall, and says nothing.

NORFOLK. Mary!

ELIZABETH. Is your sister making ready, Mary?

MARY. She was rather curious about her new dress, and so she put it on. The fashions have changed since she had a new dress.

ELIZABETH. Then she will come down?

MARY. I wonder. She was looking out the window when I left her. Does the King insist that she come down?

NORFOLK. He wants Anne to hear his song. That's all I know, niece. I'll see what happens with the King. (*He starts to go.*)

ELIZABETH. Hold him off as long as you can.

NORFOLK. I know. I will. (*Exit* C. *arch.*)

MARY. This family seems to have a strange fascination for the King. There was more than a little talk about you and him—when you were young.

ELIZABETH. Well, be sure it all came to nothing. I was seven years older than he—and married. We danced together a good deal and he had the face of an angel in those days. There was something innocent and pure about him then. He wanted to be a good king—almost a Messiah.

MARY. When he came to me first, he was still naive. He was afraid of women who might be difficult. He wanted someone to whom he could say, " Open, Sesame," and she'd open. He said, " Open Sesame " to me, and there I was.

ELIZABETH. You may yet be the mother of a king of England.

MARY. Small chance of that. And small reward in it.

ELIZABETH. My dear, it's as much as a woman ever has. (ANNE *enters down stairs.*) I like your new dress. If you wished to be beautiful in it, you could. Look your best, my dear. He's here to look at you, and he's the King. (ANNE *makes no answer.*)

MARY. Anne—if you ever go to him, lock up your heart, never surrender yourself, keep a cold reserve of hate and anger and laughter and unfaith.—For the moment you are won and conquered and a worshipper, he will give you back to yourself and walk away. He'll want no more of you. (ANNE *makes no answer.*)

ELIZABETH. You will live, Anne—you won't die. If women died as easily as men there would be no women in this world. And since you will live, you will fill your life with something. (THOMAS BOLEYN *enters* C. *arch.*)

BOLEYN. The King and his people are in the hall. Are we ready?

ELIZABETH. Quite ready, Thomas.

THOMAS. I think the King is waiting and anxious.

ELIZABETH. We are waiting. (*Enter* C. *arch in order:* 3 MUSICIANS, 3 CHOIR BOYS, WOLSEY, NORFOLK, HENRY. HENRY *carries large book with parts for* MUSICIANS *and* CHOIR.)

HENRY. Thomas—Elizabeth—Mary—Anne. I am not here tonight as your king. Something was said at one time—I forget by whom —about my bad poetry and bad music. It rankled deep—but then I saw that there was only one answer—to write great poetry and great music. And since I have a cause for anguish in my life, many songs came to me. This is only one. It may be it is not a great song, but when I hear it I know it sings what is in my heart— the pain and the loss and the parting that's like death. Here are your parts, masters. Play it as it is written, and sing it gravely, for it carries the awkward burden of a grief. (HENRY *hands music to* CHOIR *and* MUSICIANS. *All seat themselves.*)

CHOIR BOYS.

> Alas, alas,
> What shall I do
> For love, for love,
> Since now so kind I do you find—
> To keep you me unto?
> To keep you me unto?

Oh, my heart,
Oh, my heart,
My heart it is so sore,
Since I must needs from my love depart,
And know no cause therefore—
And know no cause therefore!

(*Guests applaud.* CHOIR *exits* L. 2.)

HENRY. The music will now play a sarabande of my writing. Will you dance it with me, Nan? (SERVANT *enters* R. 1 *and removes stools.* HENRY *and* ANNE *dance* C. NORFOLK *and* MARY *at* L., ELIZABETH *and* BOLEYN R. *The two couples* L. *and* R. *dance offstage after a few bars of music.* WOLSEY *exits* L. 2 *during dance.*) Nan, are you still sullen toward me?

ANNE. Northumberland is dead.

HENRY. Not by my order.

ANNE. You sent him to marry elsewhere—and it killed him.

HENRY. I couldn't let him marry you. I tried—but I couldn't.

ANNE. When I look in your face I see his murderer.

HENRY. I have learned something that makes me very humble, Nan. One cannot choose where he will love. Even a king cannot choose. I tried again and again to love elsewhere. I didn't want to come here, this year or last. But here I am. Bringing you the best I have—my music and my poetry and my love for you.

ANNE. Even if I loved you, you offer me nothing. You're not free.

HENRY. Not free?

ANNE. You are married to Catherine.

HENRY. Does that matter to a king? A king makes his own rules.

ANNE. Does he? A king or no king, if he's married he's not free.

HENRY. If you loved me you'd find me free.

ANNE. From your marriage?

HENRY. Nan, at seventeen I was hounded into marriage with Catherine, my brother's widow, for political reasons. I never loved her. I should never have married her. There's a curse on the marriage. We cannot have sons. Our sons are all born dead. There is no heir male to the English crown because of this accursed union. The kingdom faces anarchy when I die, and I face anarchy in my own life, because I have no male heir—yet because of the church and our friendship with Spain, I remain Catherine's husband. More than anything in this world I want a son, and she can't give

27

me one—yet I must not publicly put her aside. Do you understand now? This marriage is a form—important only in statecraft and churchcraft, not to you or me.

ANNE. Important or not, you can't break it. It's stronger than you are—and so you offer me nothing.

HENRY. It's not nothing, Nan. It's my whole life. I know because I tried to erase you and fill my life with other things. It won't work. I can think of nothing but you. It's not only this pain, this stitch in the side, this poetry I can't keep from writing, this music that I hear when I think of you and must write down.—I'm a man, too, Nan. I want you—and only you.—I find myself—when I'm talking to an ambassador, perhaps—I find myself thinking of you. And what am I thinking?—Of you and me playing at dog and bitch. Of you and me playing at horse and mare. Of you and me every way there is. I want to fill you up—night after night. I want to fill you with sons.

ANNE. Bastards? For they would be bastards, you know.

HENRY. If you say one more word I shall strike you. One word more.

ANNE. But it's quite obvious that if you and I had children they would be bastards. (HENRY *strikes her hard. She falls to floor.* WOLSEY, BOLEYN *and* ELIZABETH *enter*—WOLSEY *from* L. 2, BOLEYNS *from* R. 2.)

WOLSEY. Your Majesty! (ANNE *slowly gets to her feet.*)

ANNE. You have not yet understood what I mean, I think. What I am trying to tell you is that you not only offer me nothing—you offer yourself nothing. You say you want a son, an heir to the throne. You need such an heir, and the kingdom needs him. But an heir must be legitimate—not base-born—and while you are married to Catherine you can have only bastards. Fill me with as many sons as you like, you would still have no heir, and I would have—nothing.

HENRY. Would you marry me if I were free?

ANNE. You can't get free of Catherine. You know that. And I know it.

HENRY. But if I were free. Free to marry you, and would have you crowned queen of England, would you marry me? (*Long pause.*)

ANNE. Yes, if you'll make me queen of England I will marry you.

WOLSEY. My sovereign, my sovereign, we can do many things. We can shake the thrones of the Emperor and of the King of France. We can sometimes get our way even in Rome. But this we could not do. Try to divorce Catherine and you'll have the whole world against you. You'll be at war with all Europe.

HENRY.

Must I go through life, then,
dragging a sick woman—cold and sick—
blotched and middle-aged and fanatic—
who can give neither pleasure nor a living son?

WOLSEY.

My King,
any son of yours could be chosen to follow you—could be
made the heir. Even your son by a mistress.

ANNE.

He could have mistress after mistress with base-born sons—
he could make each the heir in turn!
You could even marry again—should Catherine die—
and get a legitimate son to come before mine,
and before all these! No! I will not be a mistress.
If you will marry and make me queen of England I will
give you boys in plenty,
but I will take nothing less.

WOLSEY.

Oh, my lord, I beg you—give it up!

HENRY.

I will not give it up—
I shall rid myself of Catherine,
I shall settle the question of succession once for all!
I shall make this girl queen.

WOLSEY.

My lord, my lord, don't promise this now!
It may mean more deaths than you know.
You are not yourself!

HENRY.

I shall make you queen.

WOLSEY.

She hates you! This will be a marriage of hate!

29

HENRY.

If it breaks the earth in two like an apple
and flings the halves into the void
I shall make you queen.

BLACKOUT

(*Table and chairs are removed during blackout.*)

SCENE 5

A room in Windsor Castle.
Before lights come up we hear dance music and see
shadowy figures dancing across in the darkness. NORRIS
is speaking.

NORRIS. You take four steps forward and then four steps backward and then four steps forward again. Then, if you are ablebodied—(*Lights up.*) and light on your feet, you spin around. Turn to the right always It's much easier. Watch me spin around. (*He tries.*) Well, that's not it, but it's something like it. (*On stage dancing with* NORRIS *are* SMEATON, JANE SEYMOUR, MADGE SHELTON *and the* BOLEYNS.) Shall we try it? Ready all together. Start! (*They dance.* NORFOLK *and* MORE *enter* R. 1. *Two* SERVANTS *enter* L. 2 *with table, cards, two chairs and stool. They exit* L. 2.)
MORE. What is the plan for this evening?
NORFOLK. The King and the Lady Anne will be with us soon. They are seeing the Spanish Ambassador, which is always an ordeal. Meanwhile the King prescribes amusement for us. First, Henry Norris is to teach us the Italian dance which is supposed to resemble what a man does when bitten by a tarantula.
NORRIS. That I've been trying. Shall we take a breath, everyone? (*Dance stops as* ANNE *enters* R. *arch.*)
ANNE. Oh! That Spanish Ambassador.
NORRIS. Ah! Here's the Lady Anne!
ANNE. And I've missed the dance.
NORRIS. She knows the step much better than I do. Music, please! (*They dance.*)

30

ANNE. (*When dance is over.*) Now Mark Smeaton is to teach us all a new card game which the King has invented. (*They all group around table.*)

MADGE. A card game invented by the King?

ANNE. Yes, and called King's Ransom.

SMEATON. For good reason, too. It cost me a king's ransom to learn it from him. This is how it goes. First we all ante a noble. And then I deal four cards to each player, including myself. Face up, thus.

BOLEYN. Do you need money, Jane?

JANE. No, not so far.

BOLEYN I ask because the King's treasury stands behind Lady Jane Seymour tonight.

JANE. Why does it, sir?

BOLEYN. Because you happened to sit in the King's chair. Whoever plays in the King's place may draw on the resources of the King. I have known an early to lose five hundred pounds in that seat, and walk away paying nothing because the King's treasury paid.

JANE. But if I win?

BOLEYN. Oh, what you win you keep. (HENRY *enters* L. *arch unseen.*)

SMEATON. Now that's the way to live. That's the arrangement I'd like to have with my bankers.

MORE. How men love injustice!

HENRY. Don't they? It's so much more profitable than justice. (*The court bows.*) Sit, sit, bend no more, either at the half or the quarter or the three-quarters. Relax necks, knees and middles and, if you'll be more comfortable, unbutton. I've let out a notch myself. That last portion—well, probably what I feel now is my just desert.—Did nobody understand that? Do you love justice, Sir Thomas?

MORE. Now where would I have seen it?

HENRY. Then men don't get it in this world?

MORE. They get it—always, never, or sometimes.

HENRY. "Always, never, sometimes." Let's not be serious. This used to be a dull court, religious and dutiful and dull. Now we learn to dance and there's a card game or two. And the change has come with this, my Nan, who stands before you. Come and kiss me, Nan, for you've brought gaiety into my life and the life

31

of England.—Since you don't come to kiss me I go to kiss you. (*Kisses her passionately.*)

ANNE. (*After kiss.*) Some day somebody will translate, from French into English, a book on good manners—and maybe the King of England will read it ——

HENRY. Read it, my dear, I'll write it ——

ANNE. No, Henry, but it's not only cards and dancing and amusement that make up a court. We must encourage the poets, too, and the musicians, and the philosophers. If Sir Thomas More is honored here for his *Utopia,* then he is honored through England.

HENRY. That, too, I've always wanted, you know, to feel a stirring of minds about me, to feel that my age will not go back into death without leaving a little something for men to recollect. I wish I could spend my time here, and not with legates and ambassadors and politicians, good and bad. I've been with such a set all day, and all year, and the years before—and as if that were not enough here comes another set of them, and I must send away the larks my lover has gathered and go back to quarrel among rats and dogs. (WOLSEY *and* CROMWELL *enter* R. 2.) Come in, gentlemen. Come in, my good Cardinal, you who labor while I sleep. The may-flies are about to depart and we must go to work. (*A general exodus begins to make way for business. Exit* ELIZABETH L., MADGE, NORRIS *and* SMEATON.) More, it must be four years since we sat on the palace roof together and considered the motions of the stars.

MORE. They haven't changed much, Your Majesty. (*Exit* L. 1.)

HENRY. That's the saddest subject, I know, astronomy. But very good for kings. It teaches them that kings and subjects are no different.

NORFOLK. It's a lie, Majesty. The kings can coin money and the subjects can't.

HENRY. Under heaven that means nothing, Norfolk.

NORFOLK. Over hell it means a good deal. And I'm old enough to feel pretty close to hell.—And I resent the king coining money when I can't! Especially when he cuts down the silver by half, and doubles the number of shillings in a pound! (NORFOLK *exits* C. *arch.*)

HENRY. You know, he has hold of something there. It was not quite honest, but I needed the money and I had to do it.

BOLEYN. Good night, my lord.

32

HENRY. Good night, my treasurer. There's one man who knows how desperately I had to do it. Good night, good night. (*Last of the courtiers go. Exit* BOLEYN L. 2.)

ANNE. I'll leave you two to conspire.

HENRY. Stay, my dear, stay. Help me with whatever it is.

WOLSEY. What I have to say is for Your Majesty's private ear.

HENRY. I have no private ear—not from Nan.

WOLSEY. To be frank, it could go till tomorrow. I'm sorry I interrupted. Shall we call the court back?

HENRY. On pain of my displeasure.—What did you come here to say?

WOLSEY. For the preservation of your good fortune—and that of England—I must endure your displeasure.

HENRY. It has been your habit lately to slight my wife and overlook her presence and counsel! Speak now—and before her!

WOLSEY. Why, if I must, I shall.—Our messenger returned from Rome today. We have the last word from that quarter.

HENRY. Oh ——?

WOLSEY. And not one we can welcome.

HENRY. What is it?

WOLSEY. The Pope will not annul your marriage to Catherine.

HENRY. But he must.

WOLSEY. He will not. He makes it quite definite and final.

HENRY. But what reason can he give?

WOLSEY. The reason he gives is unimportant. The true reason is that he is a prisoner, and cannot grant it.

HENRY. What kind of prisoner?

WOLSEY. An actual one. The Emperor Charles has invaded Italy and captured the Vatican. He can give orders there, and does. And the Emperor Charles is Catherine's nephew, and he doesn't want his aunt divorced from you. Pope Clement has been forbidden to favor us in the matter.

HENRY. How do you know this?

WOLSEY. From my agents in Rome.—Times will change, of course. There will be another pope; there will be another emperor. But there can be no divorce this year.

HENRY. There must be a divorce this year. Nan is with child—and her child must be heir to the throne.

WOLSEY. I warned you when you first contemplated this marriage ——

33

ANNE. It was you who came first to me, demanding me for King Henry!

WOLSEY. There was no thought of marriage at that time.

ANNE. You are a man of the church! You speak for the church!

WOLSEY. I am King Henry's minister. I speak for what can be done. I speak against what cannot.

HENRY. You will somehow get this divorce for me.

WOLSEY. My King, you and I have worked together on this. We've tried everything we could lay hands or wits on. For two years, Lady Anne, step by step, with patience and cunning and the best skill there is about us, we have tried to bring about the divorce from Catherine. I have marshalled cardinals and bishops like storm troops to assail the Pope's position. I have tried from every angle, from every direction, with money, influence, and temporal power. I have run my head against this wall like a bull in a stone barn— till there's blood dripping in my eyes and I'm worn out.

ANNE. What are we to do?

WOLSEY. Live as you were. Live as you are. Wait.

ANNE. Children don't wait for these changes among the dynasties. They come at their own time, convenient or inconvenient. They don't wait.

WOLSEY. I know no other answer. Am I dismissed, my lord?

HENRY. Yes. (WOLSEY *and* CROMWELL *bow and exit* R. *arch.*) I hoped to win suddenly and have good news for you some morning, but it hasn't come. This comes instead.—Am I forgiven, Nan?

ANNE. Is anything ever forgiven?

HENRY. Is that your answer?

ANNE. How do I know what you've agreed with Wolsey? In all your pacts with kings and princes of the whole earth, I've never known you to tell the truth—never!

HENRY. But I've told it to you!

ANNE. I thought you had. I've tried to take the place you wanted me to take—and do what must be done—because I had promised. But what I feared has come about.

HENRY. God in Heaven damn this spotted bitch! To be called a liar by my own bitch! Damn you!

ANNE. I've heard you lie to too many. You've never yet told truth when a lie would serve! And we had a bargain, remember. I said, "If you will make me queen I will marry you." But our marriage was at night and in secret; the church does not hold it valid; I am

34

not the queen, and my child will not inherit the throne! Was this planned? It's like many plans I've known you to make!

HENRY. I'll strangle you yet! I'll make an end of you!

ANNE. No doubt.

HENRY. You've lied at times! And to me! What's all this sudden passion about lying?

ANNE. I could have said, " I love you, I love you, I love you! " I didn't say it. Because I don't.—And whether you love me I don't know. You've been unfaithful to me often enough—and I've known where and with whom!

HENRY. If I have you've spoiled it for me, with your damned mocking face watching me through the walls! You spoil everything for me! Faithful—what kind of faith do you want of me? To be impotent in every bed but yours? Well, that's happened, too! They've laughed at me in their beds—more than one. Laughed at their king—and he impotent—with all but you! It's as if you were a disease within me—so that I'm in a fever when you're with me and a fever when you're absent—and it grows worse with the years that should burn it out! What more can I give, in faith or anything I have?

ANNE. What you promise! What you gave your pledged word to do!

HENRY. Anne—I have tried. Not always the right way, perhaps, but my best.

ANNE. You see—if I have a child before this divorce is granted— well, you are still as you are, untouched, but I'm not.

HENRY. I know, Anne, and it's unfair. But it's not what I meant. I meant it all quite honestly—quite as I said. I like what you've done with the court. I want you for my queen. I've lied to all the others, but not to you.—Why must she anger me? Why am I tied to this alabaster face and this pinched-up mouth and these slanted eyes?

CROMWELL. (Outside.) May I come in, Your Majesty?

HENRY. Who is it? Who disturbs here?

CROMWELL. I am the lord Cardinal's secretary, Your Majesty. My name is Thomas Cromwell.

HENRY. Stay out! No—come in. (CROMWELL approaches, R. arch, bringing two pieces of parchment.) You were just here.

CROMWELL. Yes, Majesty.

HENRY. Well, what do you want? Has the Cardinal forgotten something?

CROMWELL. He forgets nothing, my liege, except his duty to his King.

HENRY. I'm in no mood for riddles.

CROMWELL. I mean that Your Majesty may have your divorce, and the Lady Anne be crowned queen, and the child to come made heir apparent very simply. It needs only the will to do it.

HENRY. Whose will?

CROMWELL. The Cardinal's. He has something else in mind. He's playing his hand to get himself made Pope in Rome. He's not thinking of you or your divorce.

HENRY. You have been dismissed once—now once again.

ANNE. What makes you say this?

CROMWELL. I know it.

HENRY. I've worked with Wolsey. This man is mad or fanatic ——

ANNE. If the Pope will not grant the divorce—and can't grant it— how can any of these things you say be done?

CROMWELL. Forgive me, Your Majesty. I am not a fanatic, not a madman. All my life I have been an earnest student at the Inns of Court. I have read the laws of England, something which few seem to have bothered to do. There is a law of this land that makes it treason to acknowledge any higher authority than the will of the King. The church in England must grant the King a divorce if he wishes it. To maintain that the Pope may govern the King in such a matter—or in any matter—is traitorous and punishable by death. Say this to Cardinal Wolsey. He will turn white to the edge of his cape. For he too knows of this law.—To bring about all these things you wish, the King has only to appoint a new primate who will legalize his divorce and a new marriage.

HENRY. That would mean excommunication and a complete break with Rome. If there is such a law.

CROMWELL. Yes, Majesty. But there is such a law. Of that you may be sure. It is called the law of praemunire.

HENRY. I have always been a defender of the faith. And of the church. That is my greatest strength with my people. I can't change there.

CROMWELL. Allow me to say a word on that subject, Your Grace. As matters stand you are but half a king. We are only half subject to you. If you were truly king in England could a foreign prelate

36

call you to account? England is only half free. You are only half free. What the King of England wants he should have, without hindrance from abroad.

HENRY. I fear such independence might be purchased very dearly.

CROMWELL. Dearly? You have sometimes found yourself in need of money. Your Majesty.

HENRY. Well?

CROMWELL. At one stroke you could obtain your divorce and make yourself the wealthiest monarch in Europe. The monasteries of England are richer than the gold mines of the new world. Quarrel with Rome, set yourself at the head of the English church, and these riches are yours.

HENRY. You are a man without scruple, Master Cromwell.

CROMWELL. I have learned my trade, as you know, under Cardinal Wolsey. For your information I have brought with me a list of the church properties which the Cardinal has already condemned for his own use. And an itemized history of how and where he obtained the furnishings for his palace at York—as well as the titles to the estate. Cardinal Wolsey is a richer man than you, Your Majesty.

HENRY. For the third time, you are dismissed, Master Cromwell.— But I shall be able to find you if I need you?

CROMWELL. Yes, Your Majesty. (*He turns to go.*)

ANNE. I should like to see those papers.

CROMWELL. Yes, Your Majesty. (*Exit through* R. *arch.*)

ANNE. Do you think he tells the truth?

HENRY. There would be little point in his coming to us unless he told the truth.

ANNE. Is there such a law?

HENRY. I've never heard of it, but he convinces me there is.

ANNE. (*Who has parchments before her.*) The Cardinal seems to have stolen an immense amount of money.

HENRY. Doubtless he stole more than I knew. Though I'm not exactly innocent in the matter. We sometimes went halves.

ANNE. Are you also a pupil of the Cardinal's?

HENRY. I am the son of Henry the Seventh. I studied under a real master—my father. Whatever crookedness was lacking in the world when my father was born he invented before he left it. No other king of our island ever stole so widely, so successfully, so secretly—or died so rich.—And the central principle he taught me was this: Always keep the church on your side.

ANNE. Then he didn't steal from the church?

HENRY. Oh, yes. He stole from everybody. But not enough to turn it against him. I've stolen from the church, too. But not enough to turn it against me. So far.

ANNE. If this law exists—you could have the divorce, we could be married legally—and you could be richer than your father.

HENRY. I'm thinking of just that. And of my father's advice. And they pull me two ways.—I'm your prisoner, Nan. Little as I like it, I'm your prisoner, and I mean to make you my queen.— You've never told me you loved me. But if you were my queen—it would happen. You would say it, and it would be true.—And now a hatch opens. As if in the floor. It may be I could make you my queen at once. And make myself wealthy beyond hope—but I'd have to make the church my enemy.

ANNE. And you love me—not quite enough.

HENRY. Suppose I set out to make myself head of the church. I shall be opposed by many who are now my friends. They will be guilty of treason and I shall have to kill them. Those whom I like best—those who have some integrity of mind—will speak first against me. They must die. Parliament and the nation can then be bludgeoned into silence—but a lot of blood will run before they're quiet. Most of my people will hate me—and even more will hate you. Yes, I can make my Nan Queen—but we must consider the price. In how much we dare be hated. Are we willing to pay it?

ANNE. I am.

HENRY. You are new at this work, of course. You don't know quite what it means. To see blood run. If you knew I wonder if you'd still wish it.

ANNE. I am with child.

HENRY. The altar at St. Paul's will stand ankle-deep in blood. The shop-keepers will mop blood from their floors.—But it must be done if we're to marry. Well, so be it.

ANNE. Must so many die?

HENRY. Many must die. And it will look as if I had done this for money. Like my father. For the money will come to us. We'll stand ankle-deep in money, too, and I'll have my divorce and our marriage. If only you could love me a little—no, not a little—

with your whole heart—then—it wouldn't matter what happened
—or what's thought of me.
ANNE. Sometimes —— If you were ever honest—if you were ever
true ——
HENRY. Yes?
ANNE. But you never are.

DIM-OUT

(*Table, chairs and stool are removed.*)

SCENE 6

A room in York Palace.
*A few voices cry offstage. Before lights come up six
torch-bearers enter—3 from L. 1 and 3 from R. 1. They
stand at attention. The 3 R. stage cover WOLSEY, seated
at his desk from the audience.*

VOICES. Long live the new Queen! Long live Queen Anne!
A SINGLE VOICE. Long live Queen Catherine! Long live —— (*As
lights come up CROMWELL enters C. arch and crosses down R.
NORFOLK enters C. arch and stops him.*)
VOICES. Down with him! He took foreign money! Long live Queen
Anne!
NORFOLK. Master Cromwell! It seems to me the shouting for
Queen Anne was somewhat sparse along the streets—not what
you'd expect for a royal wedding and a coronation. You should
have paid them a bit and we'd have heard something really
spontaneous.
CROMWELL. They were paid.
NORFOLK. How many of them?
CROMWELL. Fifteen hundred apprentices.
NORFOLK. How much were they paid?
CROMWELL. One groat each.
NORFOLK. A groat? Man, that won't buy a whole drink of good
liquor! They should have had a silver penny apiece and they'd
have shaken the foundations! They'd have rung the bells! They'd

39

have jumped out of windows! Anyway, they'd have thrown their caps in the air! The rabble I saw must have had the mange. Their head-gear was stuck tight on their skulls and when they yelled it was more like a growl.

CROMWELL. For a half-crown each, or a whole one, they wouldn't cheer Queen Anne—not as they'd like to be cheering Queen Catherine.

NORFOLK. Why, man, have you lost faith in money? And in King Henry? They'll go along with Henry in time. Give him a few years and he'll make them love this queen as much as the first.

CROMWELL. Those that were yelling loudest were calling her a whore.

NORFOLK. Those were paid, too, Cromwell. Those were paid, too —and probably more. By the Spanish ambassador. Or by your friend Wolsey. I'm pretty sure they were paid more than you paid, because what they shouted came straight from the heart. (*Cheering begins again.*)

VOICES. God save Queen Anne! (HENRY *and* ANNE *enter from* C. *arch and pause to listen to cheering.*)

ANNE. Wasn't it rather flimsy applause?

NORFOLK. Nonsense, Your Majesty. It was what you always get in London when the folk are truly moved. It goes too deep for noise. They just stand there and weep.

ANNE. Uncle, Uncle, you're an unprincipled old sinner. There were no tears. They didn't even bother to uncover.

HENRY. Let's be thankful for the friends we have, my dear. And so, will you be happy here?

ANNE. Who else will live here?

HENRY. Only you.

ANNE. There's room for so many.

HENRY. There'll be no apartment here for anyone save you. Not even for me unless you ask me. (NORFOLK *signals* TORCHBEARERS *and they exit as they entered.* WOLSEY *is revealed, pen and paper on desk.*)

ANNE. I've never had a place that was mine.

CROMWELL. There's someone here.

WOLSEY. Ah, forgive me. Go on with whatever you have in hand, you young pepole. I'm only finishing an inventory for the new owner.

CROMWELL. Their Majesties wait for you to rise, Cardinal Wolsey.

WOLSEY. You must forgive me. I can rise only with assistance. My legs are not for dancing any more. But the inventory's ready, and now I write my name.

ANNE. I'm afraid we disturb you here.

WOLSEY. It's better that you should. Let us admit that I stole the palace in the first place and that now you take it from me. Here's the paper. I'm sorry that I can't rise and bring it to you—or kneel before you. I can only reach it out.

ANNE. I can't take it from you.

WOLSEY. Take it! Take it! My life is broke square in two. I have no use for it now, and you have. So take it! Or I'll leave it here. It's yours.

HENRY. We thought you had left for Esher.

WOLSEY. It was my intention to be gone when you came, my lord, but some friends of mine were here, and they wished to see you, and they persuaded me to stay.

HENRY. Some friends of yours?

WOLSEY. And of yours. Sir Thomas More. Bishop Fisher, and John Houghton, Prior of the Charter House in London.

HENRY. They are here?

WOLSEY. Yes. Will you see them?

HENRY. We thought to escape conferences this one day, but (*He looks at* ANNE.) kings and queens are never excused. Let them come in. (WOLSEY *claps his hands and* THREE men, SIR THOMAS MORE, BISHOP FISHER, *and* JOHN HOUGHTON, *enter from* R. *arch.* HENRY *welcomes them as they come in.*) Welcome, Sir Thomas More! Welcome, Bishop of Rochester! Welcome, Prior John Houghton! I know what you come to say, but welcome!

MORE. It's good of you to see us, Your Majesty.

HENRY. Make it plural, More. Our Majesties are both seeing you.

MORE. It's about that we wish to speak, my lord. *Bishop Fisher!*

FISHER. I have known you from a child, King Henry. I was present when you took your first three steps. You know I would not willingly say any word unpleasing to you. I have not opposed your divorce. I have not opposed your new marriage or the coronation of Queen Anne. Such things are sometimes necessary in the conduct of a state.—But you also ask that every religious in England swear fealty to you as spiritual head of the church. And I cannot accept your guidance in spiritual matters.

HENRY. But if I were not head of your church there could have been no divorce and no marriage to Anne. Anne could not have been crowned. Her child could not succeed me.

FISHER. I know that. And still I cannot accept you as my spiritual guide.

HENRY. Do you accept the church of Rome?

FISHER. Yes.

HENRY. Is the Pope moved by spiritual considerations?

FISHER. Your Majesty, I accept the spiritual authority of the church. I cannot accept your usurpation of that authority.

HENRY. Then—though I'm very sorry to lose my friend—I'm afraid you are guilty of treason and will die for it.

FISHER. If it were only I, my King, it wouldn't matter. But there are thousands of my order and of similar orders who cannot take this oath. Must they all die?

HENRY.
If they wish to die, they may. If they insist they will.
And I'll tell you why! I had no mind to cut adrift from Rome when this thing started. But I was driven to it—
by Rome—
and now the cable's cut, and we're adrift I see no anchor but the king,
and it happens I'm the king!
John Houghton, why are you here?

HOUGHTON.
I could sign everything that's asked, Your Majesty,
except the act that constitutes the king
head of the church I serve.

HENRY.
You will sign it or die.

HOUGHTON.
Then all my Charter House dies with me.

HENRY.
Have you not seen I have no alternative? It's Rome or the King! I had to choose—and now you must! Sir Thomas?

MORE.

42

I have watched you govern for many years, King Henry. You
    keep no standing army. You use your power
unjustly, illegally often, but your way
is never to go beyond what the people's will
supports. You're very shrewd
in judging what you dare do. It's as if you had
an extra sense—the king's finger—and you kept it
on the pulse of your subjects—on your whole kingdom—
and knew—before they knew—where they were going—
and how far in the year. Only this time
I don't follow you at all. How can you hope
your people will go with you ——

HENRY.

You're a great man,
Sir Thomas More, but it may be there's some truth
in that about the king's finger. They'll go with me.
The people will.

MORE.

Tell me why.

HENRY.

They don't like Rome.
They want to be free of Rome. They'll take me rather
than some foreigner over-seas. This wasn't true
ten years ago. It's beginning to be true
only now This year.

MORE.

It may be true. I don't know. I have no king's finger.
I must follow my own conscience. I can't sign.

FISHER. And I can't.

HOUGHTON. Nor I.

HENRY. I'm very sorry.

MORE. We may go?

HENRY. Yes, gentlemen. (*They start to go through* R. *arch.*) Norfolk!—(NORFOLK *gestures them off* L. 1. HENRY *stops them as
they are nearly off.*) Gentlemen, think again. You move away
from this world of your own will.

MORE. Your Majesty, it will go on without us.

HENRY. No doubt of that. Farewell, then. (*They bow out* L. 1.
NORFOLK *follows.*)

WOLSEY. Tom, will you help me up?

CROMWELL. Yes, sir. (*Helps* WOLSEY *to his feet.*)

WOLSEY. Good-bye, Your Majesties.

HENRY. Good-bye, Woolsey.

WOLSEY. Some men die for their principles, I observe, others because it's the next thing to do. (*Exit with* CROMWELL R. 1.)

ANNE. Good-bye.

HENRY. And that answers the last of them that dare speak. The rest will die silent. Anne!

ANNE. Yes?

HENRY.

> I think there's never been
> in all this world
> a king who gave so much to find his way
> to the heart of her he loved.
> Over many years,
> winter and summer, I have fought and chopped
> and hacked and stabbed my path through the jungle of laws
> and events and churchly rules—
> and the flesh of friends—
> to come to this day.
> To come to this day when I can say it's done,
> and I have earned her love.
> For all these days,
> sweet, we have lain together, and kissed and drawn
> apart from the world into a world of our own,
> but not once, not once have you said,
> " I love you."
> Did someone say to you—some time—
> " Never be all his,
> never melt to him, never forget to hate him
> at least a little—for that way you'll lose him? "

ANNE.

> I've said it to myself.

HENRY.

> Do you say it now?

ANNE.

> Yes.

HENRY.

> I see. That's what I feel. That you're never mine.

And yet—
I think I've earned your heart—all your heart—
over these years.
Yet keep it if you wish.
Only—Nan, Nan,
last night while I lay thinking of you
and couldn't sleep, and cursed myself for not sleeping,
I found myself writing the words of a lyric,
a little poem,
and trying the music for it in my mind.
It was a poem that grew from three words I heard
once, from this same Sir Thomas More, who must die,
three words, " Always, never, sometimes."
I rose and wrote the poem down, and the music,
and as I wrote I said to myself:
" Do I mean what is said by this music,
or by these words? "
And now I ask myself, " Do I mean them now? "
Here I stand, a king, with the woman I love,
planning murder for her sake,
planning to rob, lost in a copse of lies,
sweating, falling over boulders,
without a star. It's a king's life. A king lives so.
Yet the music I wrote and remember says something simple
        and sweet,
and the words are undressed truth.
Something within me drove me to write them
out of the undergrowth of sweat and lies,
looking for a star. It's that way always.
I haven't meant to do ill.
I've meant to do well.
I have known that good was better than evil,
when I've known which was evil, which was good,
but what test is there—what star, what beacon of fire?
I found it better to let all that go and write a lyric
        with music,
writing to one I loved, a woman who does not love me,
but writing truly, thus, out of myself:
        " Waking at night, I go to my window,
        Scanning the stars in a portion of sky,

Fixing on one that hangs yonder—and over
The street of the house where you lie.
If you sleep, do you dream?
If you dream, is it of me?
The clock strikes; I hear your voice in the chimes,
Repeating your words when I ask if you love me:
' Always, never, sometimes.' "

ANNE.

I love you.

HENRY.

Nan!

ANNE.

I love you. Now I know. I love you.

HENRY.

I think you mean this.

ANNE.

I've said it, and it's true.
These men who were to die, Henry—
Sir Thomas More
and all the others—they must live.

HENRY.

That was all done for you, sweet.
They shall not die. We'll lift the sentences.

ANNE.

It doesn't matter about the divorce—or the marriage—
or having this palace. Let them swear or not swear
as they like. Let Catherine keep her throne, and Mary
inherit. You love me, and I love you,
and I can say it.

HENRY.

Why can you say it?

ANNE.

Because of the things you are—
when we speak, and are close together . . .
I've been afraid to say it, afraid to be it,
but now—
Let it come, whatever it brings. I'm deep in love.
With one I hated.
Who took me anyway. Took me from my first love.
With you.

46

HENRY.

I thought you'd never say it.
Oh, if it's true, and you'll lie in my arms and love me,
Then it's a new age. Gold
or some choicer metal—or no metal at all,
but exaltation, darling. Wildfire in the air,
wildfire in the blood!
Have you room in your heart for much loving?

ANNE.

All you have.

(*They embrace.*)

CURTAIN

ACT II

SCENE 1

Lights come up first on ANNE *in solo position.* HENRY
ready as in Prologue.

ANNE.

He knew I'd love him
when once he'd made me his.
And so it was.
After that night I loved him more and more
and hated him less and less—
and I was lost.

(*Lights come up on* HENRY.)

HENRY.

What will it seem to men
I was like when I did this?
It will be written and studied.
The histories of kings are not secure.
The letters they have hidden, the secret ciphers
are unravelled and chuckled over.
" He loved her and he had her and he killed her,"
the books will say. The letters will be printed,
the stolen love-letters where I played the fool
like a country boy to his milk-maid.
There's a heart drawn
at the bottom of one, and in the heart " A. B."
laboriously written. " Henry Rex seeks
A. B., no other."
(*He prints A. B. on the air with his fingers.*)
    So the legend reads,
and will read so forever.

(*Lights go out on* HENRY.)

ANNE.

From the day he first made me his,

to the last day I made him mine,
yes,
let me set it down in numbers,
I who can count and reckon, and have the time.
Of all the days I was his and did not love him—
this; and this; and this many.
Of all the days I was his—
and he had ceased to love me—
this many; and this. In days—
it comes to a thousand days—
out of the years.
Strangely, just a thousand.
And of that thousand—
one—
when we were both in love. Only one
when our loves met, and overlapped and were both
mine and his.
When I no longer hated him, he began to hate me.
Except for that one day.
One day, out of the years.

SLOW BLACKOUT

(*Remove* ANNE'S *seat and* HENRY'S *desk. During Blackout between scenes offstage sounds. Bell.*)

      Oyez, oyez, oyez,
      Nine o'clock and all's well.
      (*Bell.*)
      Her Majesty Queen Anne
      Lies in childbed.
      Nine o'clock and all's well.

ACT II

SCENE 2

A room in York Palace.
Lights come up on ANNE *in childbed,* ELIZABETH *bending over cradle,* NORFOLK *and* MADGE *standing by.*

ELIZABETH. What beautiful little hands. What a beautiful face. Will the King be here soon?

NORFOLK. He went to change his coat, I think. We rode through miles of mud between Greenwich and here.

ELIZABETH. The King loves you a great deal, my dear.

NORRIS. (*Appearing at door* C. *arch.*) The King's at the door now, my lord. (*Exit.*)

ELIZABETH. Let me see if all's in order here.

NORFOLK. (*Speaking to* HENRY *off* C. *arch.*) It seems all's ready, Your Majesty.

HENRY. (*Entering* C. *arch.*) Nan, sweet ——

ANNE. Yes, Henry?

HENRY. Do I come too soon? Will it tire you to speak?

ANNE. No, Henry. I'm glad to see you.

HENRY. I won't say much. Nor stay long. I just want to look at you two—my queen—and my prince—my son. I shall call him Edward. It's been a lucky name for English kings. A lucky name and a great name. All my life as a King I have asked only one thing of heaven—that it grant me a son to carry on what I leave. And now heaven has given me more than I asked, for this is a handsome, bold boy's face, and already there's wit behind those eyes ——

ANNE. My lord, we have a little daughter—and her name's to be Elizabeth.

HENRY. Why did no one tell me?

NORFOLK. They're all afraid of you, my lord.

HENRY. They were wrong. Whatever happens we must look our hap in the face. Why, girl, don't look so down. If we can have a healthy girl together we can have a healthy boy together.

ANNE. I'm sorry, Henry. As if it were my fault.

HENRY. It's no fault of anyone. There must be girls as well as boys. She has a sonsie sweet face. I like her no less than I did . . . not a groat less. Get better, lass; eat well and get on your legs quickly. We'll have a good life . . . we'll let this beauty grow a foot or two, and then we'll have our son . . . and so nothing's lost. Norfolk, you said there was a sheaf of papers to sign. . . .

NORFOLK. They're on your desk, my lord.

HENRY. Right. Nan, sweet, nurse the moppet, and kiss her for me.

ANNE. Won't you kiss our little one, Henry?

50

HENRY. (*Bends down to cradle but does not kiss child.*) Come,
Duke . . . sharpen pens for me and talk high treason. It amuses
me. God keep all here. (*Exit with* NORFOLK C. *arch.*)

BLACKOUT

(*Remove bed and cradle.*)

ACT II

SCENE 3

Chapel in York Palace.
Three CHOIR BOYS *enter* R. 1. HENRY *comes down stairs.*
Projection of stained glass window on set.

HENRY. The two most important things in singing are that you remember the words, and hit the right notes. Now, sing the song
tenderly. . . . No . . . you're young, you wouldn't know about
tenderness. Sing it lightly and softly to the lady who is approach-
ing. Jane!
JANE SEYMOUR. (*Coming downstairs.*) Yes, my lord?
HENRY. They are about to sing to you, Jane.
JANE. I thank Your Majesty.
HENRY. Last night while I lay thinking, I found myself writing the
words of a lyric, a little poem, and trying the music for it in my
mind. (*He gestures to* BOYS *to sing.*)

SONG

Waking at night, I go to my window,
Scanning the stars in a portion of sky,
Fixing on one that hangs yonder, and over
The street of the house where you lie.

HENRY. (*During song.*) The music says something simple and
sweet and the words are undressed truth.

If you sleep, do you dream,
If you dream, is it of me?
The clock strikes;
I hear your voice in the chimes

51

Repeating your words
                    Always, never, sometimes.
(*Enter* ANNE C. *arch.*)
ANNE. You have written music to these words? Once before you
came to me with music. Long ago. I think I interrupt you at re-
hearsal. Forgive me. (*Seeing* JANE.) This song is not for me.
HENRY Come near me, Anne. You think me happy. I'm not happy.
(ANNE *runs offstage* C. *arch.*)

BLACKOUT

ACT II

SCENE 4

Before York Palace.
    ANNE *is winding yarn from a frame.* ELIZABETH, MADGE
    SHELTON *and* HENRY NORRIS *are in the room.* SMEATON
    *is singing to the child in the cradle. Chair and bed which
    were used in nursery scene.*
SMEATON. (*Singing.*)
                    " I had a little nut-tree,
                    Nothing would it bear,
                    But a silver nutmeg,
                    And a golden pear."
NORRIS. (*To* ANNE.) Shall we dance to it?
ANNE. Surely. (*They dance.*)
SMEATON. (*Singing.*)
                    " The king of Spain's daughter
                    Came to visit me,
                    And all for the sake
                    Of my little nut-tree."
ELIZABETH. Hush!
NORRIS. Again!
SMEATON. (*Singing.*)
                    " The king of Spain's daughter
                    Came to visit me,
                    And all for the sake
                    Of my little nut-tree."

52

ELIZABETH. She's asleep.

NORRIS. Whether to escape the singing or for delight in it, no m .n knows.

ANNE. It was well sung. But you could keep the King of Spain's daughter out of it, after this. I've had enough trouble with the King of Spain's daughter.

SMEATON. Next time I will. (NORFOLK *enters* C. *arch.*)

NORFOLK. The King's here, my chicks.

ANNE. The King of Spain?

HENRY. (*Entering with* CROMWELL, C. *arch.*) No, the King of England.

ANNE. I thought the King of Spain more likely. You stayed long at your hunting.

HENRY. We must see you.

ANNE. The Princess has grown. Would you care to look at her?

HENRY. Send your people out!

ANNE. Mark and Norris, will you carry the cradle? Mother, take Elizabeth back to her room.

ELIZABETH. Yes, dear. (SMEATON *and* NORRIS *carry the cradle off,* L. 1, *followed by* ELIZABETH *and* MADGE.) Softly now.

ANNE. Yes, King Henry, there was some question you wished to discuss with your queen?

HENRY.

> Two gentlemen of my court,
> Edward and Thomas Seymour, came to me
> an hour or two ago, demanding of me
> where they could find their sister.

ANNE.

> Does this frighten you?

HENRY.

> They are my friends.
> I have especial cause
> at this moment not to offend them.

ANNE.

> Yes, I think so.

HENRY.

> Where is Jane Seymour?

ANNE.

> In Northumberland. And a very good place for her.

HENRY.

Her brothers have made it plain
that they resent the slur you cast on her
in sending her from court.

ANNE

I don't care for her.
She has the face of a sheep. And the manners.
But not the morals.
I don't want her near me.

HENRY.

You will bring her back.

ANNE.

No, I think not.
If you want her near you, why, find a suite for her
in your own palace. This York place is mine.
You gave it to me for my own. And while
it's mine, Jane Seymour must lie elsewhere.

HENRY.

Speak to her, Norfolk.

NORFOLK.

The truth is, girl, you're on slippery ground.
More and more the common folk cry down your name.
There used to be a penalty for speaking against you.
There's none now.
And the people take advantage of it,
in the church, in the government, wherever they meet.
You have no defenders.

ANNE.

Am I at the mercy of the people?

NORFOLK.

We're all at the mercy of the people.
Sooner or later, what they want they'll have,
unless you're willing and able
to do unlimited murder on them.

ANNE.

I gave my voice for mercy.

NORFOLK.

It happens you stand for something they don't want.
They're for having the old Queen back.

HENRY.

Cromwell!

CROMWELL.

If things go as they're going,
the Commons will revolt, Your Majesty.
The divorce will be invalidated,
and your marriage also.
We've slackened our hold, and the dogs are at our throats,
yours and mine! Not the King's.

ANNE.

Why yours?

CROMWELL.

I've worked hard at suppressing monasteries
and squeezing money out of them.
You—and the King's love for you—
are slicing off England from the mother church.
We shall never be forgiven, you or I.
Nor your child.
She will not rule. Not as things go now.

HENRY.

And so, my dear,
be a little less absolute in what you'll have
and not have.

ANNE.

Jane Seymour will not couch here.

HENRY.

She will live here, among your women,
and you'll accept her.
I shall send for her to come.

ANNE.

Why, then if you need her so much
and regard me so little,
and I must take the woman into my house
against my will,
let her come, then!
But you must finish what you began with me
and left undone:
Our marriage must be valid.
If that means

that Houghton and More and Fisher must not live,
well, let them die—
let all who refuse to sign the Act of Succession
die with them!
Elizabeth must succeed you. See to that
and Jane will be accepted here.

HENRY.

She'll be accepted
because I wish it. And I'll kill no one.

ANNE.

I spared them their lives
because I loved you and you loved me! Now
you love me no more! I have nothing but my child!
Make good your promise about her!
Make her your heir!

HENRY.

You can hold me to nothing, I think.
I'll be held to nothing.

ANNE.

In that case
don't trust your lady here, within reach of my hands!

HENRY.

What would you do?

ANNE.

I'll spoil her with my hands.

HENRY.

I think not.

ANNE.

By the year when I loved elsewhere
and lost my love because you were the King;
by the time I loved no one,
but bore your weight because the earth was empty;
yes, and when I must carry your child without loving you,
because you were royal,
our child must be royal, too!
If that's not done, let Jane keep her distance from me!

HENRY.

You yourself cancelled the order for the deaths
that were needed to make your child royal.
Since then the revolt has spread. The immunity

you gave has encouraged it.
It would cost twice as many lives
now, as then, to set up our own church
and legalize what's been done.
Could you sign the death warrants that would be needed?
The infinite death warrants?

ANNE.

Oh, King of England, King of England,
you blind King!
I'd sign ten thousand to die
Rather than disinherit my blood!

HENRY.

It would need unlimited murder, as Norfolk said!
Unlimited, pitiless murder! It would mean tearing
the world apart!
To legalize a divorce and a child, and a dead marriage.

ANNE.

But you will demand it, Henry, and take it!
If it costs heads and blood and fires at Smithfield,
let the blood run and the fires burn!
It's that, or else it's my blood, and Cromwell's—
and Elizabeth's!
Cromwell knows that, your butcher-cleaver man knows that!
Send him out to implement these deaths
and let it be done quickly,
let there by no mistaking,
no leniency, no mercy!
High or low, they will sign—or depart
    without entrails!
And you will keep your word to me, unloved
though I may be!
and so I shall be Queen of this island, and
Elizabeth shall be Queen.

HENRY.

No! But you're beautiful when you're angry!
I was not wrong when I chose you queen.
Now if we had a son ——

ANNE.

What do you mean?

HENRY.

For Elizabeth, no.
For her I will not commit these murders.
But if we had a male heir—
your son and mine ——

ANNE.

I can be angrier than you've seen me yet,
and not beautiful!
I know where your heart is! It's not with me!

HENRY.

What has the heart to do
with the getting of kings?
I am not young—I am not true ——
I'm bitter and expert and aging and venomous—
not to be trusted.
Yet at this moment I want you—because of your anger
and the flash of blood in your face—
and, if you give me a prince, things may change—
even I may change!

ANNE.

No.—Not unless you kill them—
More and Houghton and Fisher
and all who will not sign—
not unless Elizabeth is your heir.

HENRY. (*To* CROMWELL.)

Put them to death, then. Go out and do it!
(CROMWELL *and* NORFOLK *exit R. arch.*)
See now. I rob and murder at your order.
And commit sacrilege.

ANNE.

You do what you wish to do and
call it my deed.
(HENRY *takes her in his arms.*)
I hate you. I hate your desire.
And mine.

HENRY.

Things could change.
Even I. I loved you once.

I saw that fire in your face.
Give me a son!

BLACKOUT

(*Remove bed, place chair for* HENRY.)

ACT II

SCENE 5

Room in Windsor Castle.
Bells chimes the hour. HENRY *sitting in his closet.* CROM-
WELL *enters* L. 1. *This scene played* C. *in a single spot*
on HENRY *at table.*

HENRY. You're late!
CROMWELL. Your Majesty, I have ill news.
HENRY. Well?
CROMWELL. The Queen is brought to bed of a son, and it's born
dead.
HENRY. A son. Born dead.
CROMWELL. Yes. (HENRY *gestures* CROMWELL *to leave, and he*
goes L. 1.)
HENRY.

A son. Born dead. Like the sons of Catherine.
Born—and a son—but cursed with the curse of God
because I've had her sister—
or because—
well, for whatever reason,
it was dead.
Oh, my God, help me! What do you want of me?
Was this girl not to your mind? Not ever?
Or am I
not to your mind?

There is a load every man lugs behind him,
heavy, invisible, sealed, concealed,
perfumed,

59

a package of dead things he drags along,
never opened
save to put in some horror of the mind—
some horror of his own doing—to seal up
and rot in secret. He pretends
there's no such thing. He tries to walk
as if he had no burden. The stench is covered
with purchased scents and flowers.
The deeds in this bag,
man and king, he utterly cancels, denies, forgets,
for they would prove him an idiot,
criminal,
sub-human.
Yet they are his.
He did them, and put them there.
And they are mine.
I did them, and put them there.
All men have done the same—
or done the like. And will.

Have you done so much better,
you out there in the future,
you whom I see with the thousand eyes, looking back
on my secret ways?
If you have, then you're young and unlucky—
it's still to come.
Or else you're old and unlucky—
it never was.

With kings as with men
there is the mask and tongue among your friends
with a ready smile and word,
and there is the hog behind the eyes, the rat
behind the tongue, the dog that runs before
and brings you after—
or lags, and holds you back.
And you obey them,
the hog, the rat, the dog.
Man, woman and child, you have obeyed them always,
and I have. The carrion and the beast

decide where we shall love, and when leave off
to love another;
not our high purpose, our resolve, our brain,
but the vermin underneath,
the unacknowledged boar, the hidden wallow,
the invisible decay.
Whatever she did, I had done first.
For when I knew for the first time she was all mine,
then, having loved her many years,
suddenly I loved her only a little,
and could look at others.
And when I felt my child move beneath her skin
I had no liking for it, and turned away—
then her lips were an overeaten plate.
Was this her blame, or mine?
Or was there blame?

BLACKOUT

(Move table and chair and add a chair R. 2.)

ACT II

Scene 6

The nursery in York Palace.
SMEATON *singing.* MADGE *and* NORRIS *playing cards.*

SMEATON. *(Singing.)*
>Sleep, little coddling,
>>Sleep, sleep warm,
>Your mother's in a taking
>>There will be a storm.

>Sleep, little hatchling,
>>Sleep, little squirrel,
>Your father's losing money,
>>There will be a quarrel.
(Enter NORFOLK *and* CROMWELL C. *arch.)*

NORFOLK. (*To* CROMWELL.) Norris and Smeaton.

CROMWELL. Yes, I know the names.

NORFOLK. First, let me speak with my niece a moment. (MADGE *exits*, R. 2.)

CROMWELL. Yes, surely.

ANNE. (*Entering* L. 2.) I kissed her good night, and she's almost asleep. She loves to hear you singing, . . . (*Sees* NORFOLK *and* CROMWELL.) Uncle Norfolk! We are honored, gentlemen, but why were you not announced?

NORFOLK. (*To* CROMWELL.) Please! (*Exit* CROMWELL, NORRIS *and* SMEATON C. *arch*.)

ANNE. Why are ye so secret, Uncle, and so black-browed?

NORFOLK. My dear, do you think you could bring yourself to live quietly somewhere—out of the kingdom—such a place as Antwerp—and not claim your rights here further?

ANNE. Why do you ask?

NORFOLK. I'm trying to be kind. If you were to make it easy to annul your marriage, why, then I could be kind.

ANNE. It's come to that, then? What would it mean for Elizabeth?

NORFOLK. She'd go to Antwerp with you.

ANNE. I'd be a mistress—a discarded mistress. With a disinherited child. No!

NORFOLK. Must I call Cromwell in again?—I'd rather not.

ANNE. Call him if you like. I'm not for Antwerp.

NORFOLK. He hoped you'd say so. He has a warrant for your arrest. There'll be a trial, girl. And I'm to sit over you as judge. I thought perhaps the arrest could be avoided.

ANNE. On what ground could I be arrested? I am the Queen. Why? what for?

NORFOLK. It's named in the warrant.

ANNE. Let me see it, then. I shall be happy to answer. (*Calling.*) Master Cromwell! No, I forgot! My lord Cromwell! (CROMWELL *enters* C. *arch*.) Let me see your warrant, if you will.

CROMWELL. Yes, Your Majesty.

ANNE. For—adultery? Adultery? With whom?

CROMWELL. With those found in your chambers with you. And with three others.

ANNE. . . . All men will know this is untrue.

CROMWELL. You have her promise to leave the kingdom?

NORFOLK. No.

CROMWELL. Come in, gentlemen. (NORRIS *and* SMEATON *enter* C. *arch, also two Bailiffs,* R. 2 *and* L. 2.) You are under arrest. The Queen is under arrest.

NORFOLK. Niece, it's pure nonsense, but—here it is.

CROMWELL. You will take a few things and come.

ANNE. But the child?

CROMWELL. You will leave her with your women.

ANNE. Then—what women may I take with me?

CROMWELL. You will be furnished with attendants at the Tower.

SMEATON. We go to the Tower, too?

CROMWELL. You go to the Tower. (*All go out* C. *arch.*)

BLACKOUT

(*In darkness between scenes the following.*)

CROMWELL. Answer.

VOICE. Oh, God! Help me!

CROMWELL. Answer!!

VOICE. Yes, I confess, I confess!

CROMWELL. With the Queen?

VOICE. Yes, with the Queen!

CROMWELL. Take him down! (*Calling.*) Henry Norris! (*The effect must be as of one being tortured to confess.*)

ACT II

SCENE 7

The Town Lights come up on NORFOLK, *seated as a judge. A Clerk below him, writing.* HENRY NORRIS *in witness-stand.* CROMWELL *acting as prosecutor.* ANNE *sitting on a stool as defendant. A Bailiff stands behind* NORRIS.

CROMWELL. (*As the lights come up.*) I ask you this question for the last time, Henry Norris, and I warn you that there is mercy in this court only for those who tell truth. What were your relations with the Queen?

NORRIS. Master Cromwell! I have always honored Her Majesty, Queen Anne, for her known and unquestioned virtue. Whoever has slandered her enough to say there was ever a breach of wrong between her and me—he lies, no matter who he is, or where.

CROMWELL. Your guilt is open and known, sir. You will find it useless to deny it.

NORRIS. You have brought no witnesses against me. I am unjustly accused in this star-chamber and quite guiltless—and I believe the Queen to be quite as guiltless as I am.

CROMWELL. Remove Henry Norris, and bring in Mark Smeaton.

NORRIS. Lord Norfolk, this is no just procedure! Do you continue to lend it your countenance?

NORFOLK. Every man to his own conscience, lad.

NORRIS. God keep me from yours!

NORFOLK. That He will do.

NORRIS. The one witness the prosecution has found is a loose-mouthed woman of sinister reputation! The Queen has denied her guilt. The men accused with her deny their guilt and hers—in spite of torture, bribes and promises of acquittal!

NORFOLK. Let us proceed with the case. The next witness. (NORRIS *is led out by a Bailiff,* R. 1. SMEATON *is led in* R. 1 *by another Bailiff. The mark of a rope is around his brows.*)

CROMWELL. Swear him. (BAILIFF *puts* SMEATON'S *hand on a Bible.*)

BAILIFF. Do you swear to tell truth at this trial?

SMEATON. Yes. (BAILIFF *takes Bible away.*)

CROMWELL. Again I warn you, Mark Smeaton, that there will be mercy only for those who tell truth. What were your relations with the woman who sits here, the former Queen Anne?

SMEATON. My lord ——

CROMWELL. Do you wish to spend another half hour with the executioner?

SMEATON. No.

CROMWELL. Then truthfully. Did you have carnal relations with Queen Anne? Answer!

SMEATON. (*Desperately.*) Yes.

CROMWELL. Did you answer "yes"?

SMEATON. (*Low.*) Yes.

CROMWELL. He confesses it. (*To* CLERK.) Be sure this is written.

(*To* SMEATON.) You had relations with the Queen at sundry times and places?

SMEATON. Yes.

CROMWELL. Why, now you begin to talk like a man. Now we begin to think well of you, and you shall be treated like a man.

ANNE. My lord! My lord of Norfolk!

NORFOLK. Yes, Lady Anne?

ANNE. May I question this man—Mark Smeaton?

NORFOLK. Why do you wish to question him?

ANNE. You know this is not a trial, Uncle Norfolk! It's like an evil dream, with no witnesses, no defense for the accused, no sifting of evidence, no waft of air from outside, and yet I'm being tried here for my life—and five men are being tried! Since no man speaks for me or examines for me, let me speak and examine for myself!

NORFOLK. Lord Cromwell examines for you.

ANNE. He! He brought me here! He is my accuser!

NORFOLK. Why, let her question Mark Smeaton.

ANNE. Thank you, my lord. Mark, look at me! I know well you've been tortured, but you know it's not true—what you've said about you and me. Why do you say it?

SMEATON. (*Low.*) It is true.

CROMWELL. (*To* CLERK.) Write that. He says it is true. (HENRY *appears at top of stairs unseen.*)

ANNE. Mark, you poor lad, I've been at the other end of the process, and I know the wiles they use on the rats and rabbits they catch in their trap. I know why you've changed your mind and say now that I'm guilty. They've promised you your life.

CROMWELL. He's said it three times now. We have our evidence.

ANNE. Isn't it better, if we're to die, that we die with the truth on our lips? You can't save me or save yourself, but you will save something if you refuse to utter a falsehood with the last breath you have. It's a pernicious falsehood, and its influence will go on forever. It's the word you will be remembered for.

SMEATON. (*Desperate.*) It's not a falsehood. It's true. I'm guilty! I was guilty with the Queen! Let me go! Let me go! I was guilty! The Queen was guilty! Let me go free!

ANNE. Mark! Mark! Who do you say it for? For Cromwell, there, this hollow-ground death's man? He's promised life to uncounted monks and men—and seen them hastily buried. It's his trade. He's done it for me—to my shame.

SMEATON. (*Falls in front of* NORFOLK.) She came to my bed! I swear it!

ANNE. Mark! Mark!

CROMWELL. (BAILIFF *starts to carry* SMEATON *off* R.; *is stopped by* HENRY.) Take him out!

HENRY. (*Who has been hidden on stairs.*) Mark Smeaton!

ANNE. Ah! He who sees everything, who knows everything! The King!

HENRY. (*To* SMEATON.) You say the Queen came to your bed? When? How many times?

SMEATON. (*Not looking up.*) Many times.

HENRY. When was this?

SMEATON. I don't remember.

HENRY. You will remember! Call it to mind, man, or you'll speak with those who can jog your memory! When did this happen? Where?

SMEATON. At York place.

HENRY. You lie. It could never have happened at York place—for you slept in a room with two others!

SMEATON. No, no, it was at Windsor!

HENRY. Fool! She went to Windsor only with me. Can you find no better lie?

SMEATON. It was many places! She came to my bed! It was wherever you like, whenever you like! Oh, God help me, let me go! Let me go free!

HENRY. Did Cromwell promise you your life if you said this?

CROMWELL. My lord!

HENRY. Cease this pen-scratching! Answer me! Did he say you would live?

SMEATON. Yes.

HENRY. He lied to you. You're to die, musician. Say what you like, you're to die! Speak now without lying, for it gains you nothing!

SMEATON. Why am I to die?

HENRY. You're to die in any case, whatever's said from here on. And now that you know that, what happened between you and the Queen?

SMEATON. (*Coming to himself.*) Between the Queen and me?

66

Nothing. She was kind and pleasant and just. I wouldn't hurt her. But they've broken me with ropes and irons—and wooden wedges. (*He faints.*)

HENRY. Take him out. (BAILIFF *leads* SMEATON *out* R. 1. *To* CROMWELL.) Do you convict on such testimony?

CROMWELL. There is no lack of testimony, Your Majesty. It's not this man, not any one man, five men have sworn to it.

HENRY. And yet it could be true. (*To* ANNE.) You were no virgin when I met you first. You told me as much. You knew what it was to have men.

ANNE. Have you stepped into your own trap, my lord? Any evidence you have against me you yourself bought and paid for. Do you now begin to believe it?

HENRY. (*Looks at her steadily for a moment, then turns.*) I was a fool to come here!

ANNE. Why did you come?

HENRY. Because I wanted to know! Because I wanted to know! And still I don't know! And no man ever knows!

ANNE. Whether I was unfaithful to you?

HENRY. Yes! Just that! Whether you were unfaithful to me while I loved you! But I'll never know! Whether you say aye or no. I won't be sure either way! Fool that I am! That all men are!

ANNE.
There are fools and fools, King Henry.
You've shut me up here
to be tried for adultery and treason toward you.
You've done this because you love elsewhere—
and I know it ——
But now you come here
to make sure whether there were truly adultery,
because that would touch your manhood—
or your pride!
And you wait and listen, a cat in a corner,
watching the pet mouse before it dies.
And then you come out—to make sure!
And, oh fool of fools,
even so, my heart and my eyes
are glad of you.
Fool of all women that I am,
I'm glad of you here!

67

Go then. Keep your pride of manhood.
You know about me now.

HENRY.

Nan ——

ANNE.

Mind, I ask no pity of you ——

HENRY.

Nan! I have no wish to harm you.
I am much moved by what you said. I'd rather
a year cut out of my life than do you wrong.
After those words of yours.
Did you say—
did you say truly, you were glad of me here?

ANNE.

I won't say it again.
But I did say it.
And it was true.

HENRY.

Then,
let's do all this gently, Nan,
for old times' sake.
I have to prove that I can father a king
to follow me.
You and I,
we'll not have a son now.
God has spoken there.
Go quietly. Sign the nullification.

ANNE.

No.
We were king and queen, man and wife together. I
keep that.
Take it from me as best you can.

HENRY.

You do leave no choice.

ANNE.

Would you let this grind on the way it's going?

HENRY.

You would, if it served your purpose.

ANNE.

I?

68

HENRY.

I remember
Your saying, " Let them die," upon a time.
You've forgotten it, no doubt.

ANNE.

No, I did say it.
These things look different from the other end.
If I'd known then what I feel now—
I couldn't have done it.

HENRY.

No.

ANNE.

I've been your wife.
Could you do it to me?

HENRY.

Yes. If you stood in my way.
Defiantly. As you do.

ANNE.

You're not old. You've been long a king.
But you're still young and could change.
You said—on that one day when we loved each other—
you remember—that one day when I loved you
and you loved me—that you would change—would
        seek justice—
would be such a king as men had hoped you'd be
when you came to the throne?
It's not too late for that.
Only if you harden in your mind toward me,
and say, it's nothing, like the other rats and rabbits
let her be cut and torn and buried—
then I think
it will be indeed too late.
The king—the great king
you might have been, will have died in you.

HENRY.

Now I'll tell you truly.
I do want to begin again.
And I can't with you.
You brought me into blood—that bloody business
of the death of More and all the pitiful folk

who were like him and wouldn't sign.
Your hand was to that. It's blood-stained.

ANNE.

And yours? Not yours?
Will you give back what you stole from the monasteries,
and the men executed?
Will you resume with Rome?
When you do that I'll take your word again,
But you won't do it.
And what you truly want—
you may not know it—
Is a fresh, frail, innocent maid who'll make you feel
fresh and innocent again,
and young again;
Jane Seymour is the name. It could be anyone.
Only virginal and sweet. And when you've had her
you'll want someone else.

HENRY.

It's not true.

ANNE.

Meanwhile, to get her,
you'll murder if you must.

HENRY. (*Angry.*)

Why, then you've decided.—And so have I.

(*He starts away.*)

ANNE. (*Flashing out.*)

Before you go, perhaps
You should hear one thing—
I lied to you.
I loved you, but I lied to you! I was untrue!
Untrue with many!

HENRY.

This is a lie.

ANNE.

Is it? Take it to your grave! Believe it!
I was untrue!

HENRY.

Why, then, it's settled.
You asked for it. You shall have it.

70

ANNE.

Quite correct.

Only what I take to my grave you take to yours!

With many! Not with one! Many!

HENRY. (*To* NORFOLK.)

She's guilty!

Proceed with this mummery.

(*He turns to go.*)

CROMWELL.

May we have your signature, my lord?

HENRY.

Lend me your pen.

(*He takes* CLERK'S *pen from his hand, pulls a paper from his pocket, and sits to write on* CLERK'S *seat.* CLERK *exits L. 2. Lights dim on all those present save* HENRY *and* ANNE.)

She lies, she lies. She was not unfaithful to me.

And yet—if she were—

If she lies, let her die for lying!

Let her die.

(*He writes.*)

Oh, God, oh, God,

sometimes I seem to sit in a motionless dream,

and watch while I do a horrible thing

and know that I do it,

and all the clocks in all the world stand still—

waiting.

What is she thinking in this halted interval

while no mote falls through the shaft of sunlight

and no man takes a breath?

(*Light on* HENRY *goes out.*)

ANNE.

I've never thought what it was like to die.

To become meat that rots. Then food for shrubs,

and the long roots of vines.

The grape could reach me.

I may make him drunk before many years.

Some one told me the story

of the homely daughter of Sir Thomas More,

climbing at night up the trestles of London Bridge

where they'd stuck her father's head on a spike,

and hunting among the stinking and bloody heads,
of criminals, still she found her father's head,
his beard matted and hard with blood.
And climbing down with it, and taking it home.
To bury in the garden, perhaps.
Would they fix my head up on London Bridge?
No. Even Henry would object to that.
I've been his queen. He's kissed my lips.
He wouldn't want it. I'll lie in lead—or brass.
    Meat. Dead meat.
But if my head were on the Bridge he wouldn't climb
    to take it down.
Nobody'd climb for me. I could stay and face up the
    river,
and my long hair blow out and tangle round
the spikes—and my small neck.
Till the sea birds took me,
and there was nothing but a wisp of hair
and a cup of bone.
I must think of something to say when the time comes.
If I could say it—with the axe edge toward me,
Could I do it? Could I lay my head down—
and smile, and speak? Till the blow comes?
They say it's subtle. It doesn't hurt. There's no time.
No time. That's the end of time.

(*All lights up.*)

HENRY. (*Rising, paper in his hands.*)
    Shall I tear this?

ANNE.

    No.
Go your way, and I'll go mine.
You to your death, and I to my expiation.
For there is such a thing as expiation.
It involves dying to live.

HENRY.

    Death is a thing the coroner can see.
I'll stick by that.

ANNE.

    A coroner wouldn't know you died young, Henry.
And yet you did.

HENRY. (*Turning away.*)

> Burn these records!

(*He kicks* CLERK'S *book, which lies on the floor, and goes out G. arch.*)

BLACKOUT

(*Remove all furniture.*)

ACT II

SCENE 8

> Same as Prologue.
> HENRY *seated at desk. Bell tolls the hour.*

HENRY.

> I've worked all night.
> There's light in the window.
> They say you need less sleep as you grow older.
> Or more.
> One or the other. This night I've had none.
> (*Puts out a hand.*)
> Yet my hand's steady as a tree.
> And the writing's firm as a boy's.
> This is the morning she's to die. I'd almost forgotten.
> That would have shaken me, ten years ago.
> Not now.
> (*He lays quill down.*)
> I need a new pen.
> (*He takes up the penknife and begins to cut a new quill with practiced hand. The boom of a single cannon is heard.*)
> Nan is dead. Well, so much for Nan. That's over.
> (*He pares tranquilly at the quill. Suddenly there's blood on the paper and on his hands. He throws down knife and quill, stanching blood with a handkerchief.*)
> And so your hands are steady, are they?
> Open the bag you lug behind you, Henry.
> Put in Nan's head.

Nan's head.
and her eyes, and the lips you kissed.
Wherever you go they'll follow after you now.
Her perfume will linger
in every room you enter, and the stench
of her death will drive it out.
Get on with your work.
These are not empty things you do.
(ANNE *appears* R. C.)
It's Nan.
No doubt I'll sometimes see you when I'm alone.
Whenever I'm weary
and the old ways and days come back to me,
and the things you said.
But it will wear out, will erase
like a path nobody walks on.—Why do you smile?
—I can hear you saying, " Nothing's ever forgiven,
nothing's ever forgotten or erased,—
nothing can ever be put back the way it was.
The limb that was cut from Rome won't graft
        to that trunk again."
What we were will be permanent in England;
It may be then what we were will be permanent in me.
It may be all other women will be shadows
and I'll be angered,
and turn from one white face to another,
striking left and right like an angry snake
spewing venom,
striking down,
till I'm old and drained of venom.
It may be I shall seek you forever down the long
        corridors of air,
finding them empty, hearing only echoes.
It would have been easier to forget you living
than to forget you dead.

Slow Blackout

CURTAIN

74

PROPERTY LIST

Regarding the basic furniture properties, see Note on Production. The present includes only the basic properties aside from the desks, chairs, tables, bed, and cradle indicated in the script.

Quill pen and parchment (Henry)
Anne's necklace
Large music book with music parts
2 packs of playing cards
2 pieces of parchment
6 torches
Quill pen and parchment (Wolsey)
Yarn and yarn frame
Quill pen and parchment (for Clerk of the Court)
Bible
Parchment or paper (Henry)
Pen knife (for Henry)
Handkerchief (for Henry)

NEW PLAYS

★ **MOTHERHOOD OUT LOUD by Leslie Ayvazian, Brooke Berman, David Cale, Jessica Goldberg, Beth Henley, Lameece Issaq, Claire LaZebnik, Lisa Loomer, Michele Lowe, Marco Pennette, Theresa Rebeck, Luanne Rice, Annie Weisman and Cheryl L. West, conceived by Susan R. Rose and Joan Stein.** When entrusting the subject of motherhood to such a dazzling collection of celebrated American writers, what results is a joyous, moving, hilarious, and altogether thrilling theatrical event. "Never fails to strike both the funny bone and the heart." *–BackStage.* "Packed with wisdom, laughter, and plenty of wry surprises." *–TheaterMania.* [1M, 3W] ISBN: 978-0-8222-2589-8

★ **COCK by Mike Bartlett.** When John takes a break from his boyfriend, he accidentally meets the girl of his dreams. Filled with guilt and indecision, he decides there is only one way to straighten this out. "[A] brilliant and blackly hilarious feat of provocation." *–Independent.* "A smart, prickly and rewarding view of sexual and emotional confusion." *–Evening Standard.* [3M, 1W] ISBN: 978-0-8222-2766-3

★ **F. Scott Fitzgerald's THE GREAT GATSBY adapted for the stage by Simon Levy.** Jay Gatsby, a self-made millionaire, passionately pursues the elusive Daisy Buchanan. Nick Carraway, a young newcomer to Long Island, is drawn into their world of obsession, greed and danger. "Levy's combination of narration, dialogue and action delivers most of what is best in the novel." *–Seattle Post-Intelligencer.* "A beautifully crafted interpretation of the 1925 novel which defined the Jazz Age." *–London Free Press.* [5M, 4W] ISBN: 978-0-8222-2727-4

★ **LONELY, I'M NOT by Paul Weitz.** At an age when most people are discovering what they want to do with their lives, Porter has been married and divorced, earned seven figures as a corporate "ninja," and had a nervous breakdown. It's been four years since he's had a job or a date, and he's decided to give life another shot. "Critic's pick!" *–NY Times.* "An enjoyable ride." *–NY Daily News.* [3M, 3W] ISBN: 978-0-8222-2734-2

★ **ASUNCION by Jesse Eisenberg.** Edgar and Vinny are not racist. In fact, Edgar maintains a blog condemning American imperialism, and Vinny is three-quarters into a Ph.D. in Black Studies. When Asuncion becomes their new roommate, the boys have a perfect opportunity to demonstrate how open-minded they truly are. "Mr. Eisenberg writes lively dialogue that strikes plenty of comic sparks." *–NY Times.* "An almost ridiculously enjoyable portrait of slacker trauma among would-be intellectuals." *–Newsday.* [2M, 2W] ISBN: 978-0-8222-2630-7

DRAMATISTS PLAY SERVICE, INC.
440 Park Avenue South, New York, NY 10016 212-683-8960 Fax 212-213-1539
postmaster@dramatists.com www.dramatists.com

NEW PLAYS

★ **THE PICTURE OF DORIAN GRAY by Roberto Aguirre-Sacasa, based on the novel by Oscar Wilde.** Preternaturally handsome Dorian Gray has his portrait painted by his college classmate Basil Hallwood. When their mutual friend Henry Wotton offers to include it in a show, Dorian makes a fateful wish—that his portrait should grow old instead of him—and strikes an unspeakable bargain with the devil. [5M, 2W] ISBN: 978-0-8222-2590-4

★ **THE LYONS by Nicky Silver.** As Ben Lyons lies dying, it becomes clear that he and his wife have been at war for many years, and his impending demise has brought no relief. When they're joined by their children all efforts at a sentimental goodbye to the dying patriarch are soon abandoned. "Hilariously frank, clear-sighted, compassionate and forgiving." –*NY Times.* "Mordant, dark and rich." –*Associated Press.* [3M, 3W] ISBN: 978-0-8222-2659-8

★ **STANDING ON CEREMONY by Mo Gaffney, Jordan Harrison, Moisés Kaufman, Neil LaBute, Wendy MacLeod, José Rivera, Paul Rudnick, and Doug Wright, conceived by Brian Shnipper.** Witty, warm and occasionally wacky, these plays are vows to the blessings of equality, the universal challenges of relationships and the often hilarious power of love. "CEREMONY puts a human face on a hot-button issue and delivers laughter and tears rather than propaganda." –*BackStage.* [3M, 3W] ISBN: 978-0-8222-2654-3

★ **ONE ARM by Moisés Kaufman, based on the short story and screenplay by Tennessee Williams.** Ollie joins the Navy and becomes the lightweight boxing champion of the Pacific Fleet. Soon after, he loses his arm in a car accident, and he turns to hustling to survive. "[A] fast, fierce, brutally beautiful stage adaptation." –*NY Magazine.* "A fascinatingly lurid, provocative and fatalistic piece of theater." –*Variety.* [7M, 1W] ISBN: 978-0-8222-2564-5

★ **AN ILIAD by Lisa Peterson and Denis O'Hare.** A modern-day retelling of Homer's classic. Poetry and humor, the ancient tale of the Trojan War and the modern world collide in this captivating theatrical experience. "Shocking, glorious, primal and deeply satisfying." –*Time Out NY.* "Explosive, altogether breathtaking." –*Chicago Sun-Times.* [1M] ISBN: 978-0-8222-2687-1

★ **THE COLUMNIST by David Auburn.** At the height of the Cold War, Joe Alsop is the nation's most influential journalist, beloved, feared and courted by the Washington world. But as the '60s dawn and America undergoes dizzying change, the intense political dramas Joe is embroiled in become deeply personal as well. "Intensely satisfying." –*Bloomberg News.* [5M, 2W] ISBN: 978-0-8222-2699-4

DRAMATISTS PLAY SERVICE, INC.
440 Park Avenue South, New York, NY 10016 212-683-8960 Fax 212-213-1539
postmaster@dramatists.com www.dramatists.com